NEW GENDER AGENDA
Why women still want more

edited by
Anna Coote

30-32 Southampton St
London WC2E 7RA
Tel: 020 7470 6100
Fax: 020 7470 6111
postmaster@ippr.org.uk
www.ippr.org.uk
Registered charity 800065

This book is published in association with the Fawcett Society and the Fabian Society.

The Institute for Public Policy Research is an independent charity whose purpose is to contribute to public understanding of social, economic and political questions through research, discussion and publication. It was established in 1988 by leading figures in the academic, business and trade-union communities to provide an alternative to the free market think tanks.

IPPR's research agenda reflects the challenges facing Britain and Europe. Current programmes cover the areas of economic and industrial policy, Europe, governmental reform, human rights, defence, social policy, the environment and media issues.

Besides its programme of research and publication, IPPR also provides a forum for political and trade union leaders, academic experts and those from business, finance, government and the media, to meet and discuss issues of common concern.

Production & design by **EMPHASIS**
ISBN 1 86030 120 7
© IPPR 2000
Printed and bound in Great Britain by Biddles Ltd, *www.biddles.co.uk*

Contents

Acknowledgements

Helen Wilkinson was to have been the co-editor of this volume but was obliged to stand down because of unexpected time constraints. I am grateful for her considerable help in commissioning many of the chapters and for her support for the project throughout. Very special thanks to Harriet Harman for her unflagging enthusiasm and invaluable encouragement, to Mary Ann Stephenson and Jane Franklin who helped to shape the collection, Lisa Harker for her thoughtful reading and to Helena Scott for her forbearance. Finally, many thanks to all the contributors and to Jim Godfrey, Matthew Taylor and Liz Kendall at IPPR, to Mary-Ann Stephenson at the Fawcett Society and to Michael Jacobs at the Fabian Society.

About the contributors

Wendy Alexander is the Minister for Communities and MSP for Paisley North. She was previously a special adviser to the Secretary of State for Scotland and a Global Management Consultant. She graduated from Glasgow and Warwick Universities and has an MBA from INSEAD business school.

Yasmin Alibhai-Brown is an award winning journalist and broadcaster with a weekly column in *The Independent*. She is a senior Research Fellow at the Foreign Policy Centre and author of *True Colours* (IPPR), *Who Do We Think We Are? Imagining the New Britain* and *After Multiculturalism* (Foreign Policy Centre).

Melissa Benn is a journalist, novelist, essayist, broadcaster and teacher. Her most recent non-fiction book is *Madonna and Child: Towards a New Politics of Motherhood* (Vintage1999).

Ian Christie is associate director of the economic development consultancy The Local Futures Group and is also senior research associate with the think-tank Demos. His recent publications include *Sustaining Europe* (Green Alliance, 1999) and *Managing Sustainable Development* with Michael Carley (Earthscan, 2000).

Anna Coote is Director of the Public Health Programme at the King's Fund. She was formerly Deputy Director of IPPR where she led the Institute's ground-breaking work on health and social policy, and on citizens' juries and deliberative public involvement. She has been adviser to the Minister for Women (1997-8); a Senior Lecturer in Media and Communications at Goldsmiths College, London University (1991-3); a producer and editor of current affairs and documentaries for Channel

Four TV (1982-9); Deputy Editor of the *New Statesman* (1978-82), and a journalist and broadcaster.

Val Feld was Wales director of the Equal Opportunities Commission before becoming Labour member for Swansea East in the Welsh Assembly. She was closely involved in the equal representation campaign.

Jane Franklin is a Research Fellow at South Bank University. Her publications include *Equality* (IPPR, 1997), *The Politics of Risk Society* (Polity, 1998), *Social Policy and Social Justice* (Polity, 1998).

Diane Gardner is a graduate student in Politics at Nuffield College, Oxford, and a graduate of the University of Auckland. Her specialism is political philosophy. She is currently working to complete her D Phil on the value of autonomy and the (non-) justifiability of paternalism.

Harriet Harman was elected MP for Camberwell and Peckham in a by-election in 1982. In July 1984 she was appointed as Labour Front-bench Spokesperson for Social Services. Following the 1987 election she became Labour Front-bench Spokesperson on Health. After the 1992 election she was elected to Labour's Shadow Cabinet and appointed Shadow Chief Secretary to the Treasury. In 1997 she became Secretary of State for Social Security and Minister for Women. Throughout her career she has campaigned on childcare, domestic violence and equality for women. Harriet Harman is currently Chair of the Childcare Commission which is due to present its findings to the Government early next year.

Patricia Hewitt was elected as MP for Leicester West in May 1997. She is Minister for Small Business and e-Commerce at the Department of Trade and Industry, having previously been Economic Secretary at the Treasury. Before entering Parliament, she was Director of Research at Andersen Consulting, having previously been Deputy Director of the Institute for Public Policy Research and Policy Co-ordinator to Rt Hon Neil Kinnock MP when he was Leader of the Opposition.

Michael Jacobs is General Secretary of the Fabian Society. An economist, he is the author of *The Green Economy* (Pluto Press 1991) and *The Politics of the Real World* (Earthscan 1996). He is Secretary to the Fabian Society's Commission on Taxation and Citizenship and principal author of its report *Paying for Progress, A New Politics of Tax* (October 2000).

Alex Jones graduated from Pembroke College, Cambridge in Social and Political Sciences, where she specialised in political theory, in 1999.

Ruth Kelly was elected as the Labour MP for Bolton West in May 1997 and became parliamentary private secretary to Agriculture Minister Nick Brown after serving on the Treasury Select Committee. Previously an economics writer for the *Guardian* newspaper, she has also worked for the Bank of England.

Liz Kendall is the Senior Research Fellow in Health Policy at IPPR. She was previously the Fellow on the Public Health Programme at the King's Fund health charity. Between 1996 and 98 she was a Political Adviser to Harriet Harman, MP.

Deborah Mattinson is Chair of Opinion Leader Research, a leading market research organisation. She is an expert in social and corporate research based strategy and has advised the Labour Party since 1985.

Anne Perkins was a political correspondent for Channel Four News, the BBC and the *Guardian*. Now a freelance political writer, she is working on a biography of Barbara Castle.

Anne Phillips is Professor of Gender Theory and Director at the Gender Institute at the London School of Economics. Her publications include *Engendering Democracy* (Polity, 1991); *The Politics of Presence: The Political Representation of Gender, Ethnicity and Race* (OUP, 1995) and *Which Equalities Matter?* (Polity, 1999).

Mary-Ann Stephenson is the Director of the Fawcett Society, the leading organisation campaigning for equality between women and men in the UK. She has worked at Fawcett since 1996, working as Campaigns Manager before being appointed Director in May 1999. Prior to Fawcett Mary-Ann worked at Liberty (the National Council for Civil Liberties) and the international human rights organisation, Article 19. She is a member of the Management Board of New Ways to Work and the Steering Committee of the Women's National Commission.

Matthew Taylor is Director of the IPPR. Until December 1998 he was Assistant General Secretary for the Labour Party. During the 1997 General election he was Labour's Director of Policy and a member of the Party's central election strategy team. He was appointed to the Labour party in 1994 to establish Labour's rebuttal operation. His activities before the Labour Party included being a county councillor, a parliamentary candidate, a university research fellow and the director of a unit monitoring policy in the health service.

Lucy Ward is a political correspondent for *The Guardian*. She started out in journalism in 1992 at the Bradford *Telegraph & Argus*, before moving to the *Times*

Educational Supplement and then the *Independent*, where she was education correspondent.

Stuart White is Tutorial Fellow in Politics at Jesus College, Oxford. His research interests lie mainly in the area of political theory. He is the editor of *New Labour: The Progressive Future?* (Macmillan, forthcoming) and is currently working to complete a book on justice and social policy provisionally entitled *Civic Egalitarianism: A Theory of Economic Citizenship.*

Introduction
Anna Coote

It is time to take stock of the troubled relationship between women's politics and New Labour in government. Anyone looking back from a later period in our history may judge the 'millennium years' when Tony Blair was Prime Minister to have been a high point. Like the mid-1970s, it may be seen as one of those rare moments when the aspirations of women and government coincided, when laws and benefits and other helpful measures were heaped upon us, and life was never quite the same again.

Yet three years into the New Labour government, there is a sense of unease and dissatisfaction. Many of the women who worked hard to modernise and feminise the Labour Party in opposition, and to dislodge the Conservatives from Downing Street, witnessed the Blair landslide in 1997 with burgeoning hopes. Would women's voices at last be heard and heeded? Would women now have a chance to share power on equal terms? Would our needs be acknowledged and addressed? Undoubtedly, the outlook is far, far better than under the last government. But there is a widely shared view that, if this is as good as it gets, it is not good enough. Nor is the feeling confined to political elites. According to an ICM poll in the *Guardian*, Labour's lead among women voters aged 18-35 plummeted from a 40-point lead over the Conservatives in early 1999 to 21 points in July 2000. (The party's lead among younger men meanwhile was never so high and declined by only two points from 23 to 21.) What is going on? And what lessons can be learned for the next election and the next parliament?

This book was conceived in a seminar series run by the Fawcett Society in the summer and autumn of 1999 and designed to bring together different generations of feminists – veterans of the 1970s liberation movement and younger women who had grown up in the Thatcher years. Although we had often heard that we were at odds with each other, we found we had a lot in common. We shared a sense of unfulfilled promise – and a need to understand. Why had the triumph of 100 women in parliament become a sorry joke? Why had Downing Street begun to feel like an exclusive boys' club? Why had feminism become a dirty word, even with the newly appointed Minister for Women? And why had a party that owed its electoral victory largely to women apparently turned its back on gender politics? We shared a view that feminism was essential to the process of modernisation, since it was about bringing politics into line with changing circumstances, attitudes and relationships. We also shared a conviction that the Government ignored at its peril the voices and experience of more than half the electorate. It needed women, more than it realised, both to pursue its policy goals and to fulfil its political ambitions.

Four broad themes emerge from the chapters that follow. The first concerns the implications for women of New Labour's particular brand of 'big tent' politics. The second is concerned with contemporary feminism and democracy, and how women make their presence felt in the political sphere. The third addresses the apparently eternal and inevitably central problem of juggling work and family. The final theme is about how women's interests and experience, as well as feminist politics, shape the wider policy agenda.

Blair's big tent

Renaming the party 'New Labour' signalled a determination to break with the past and to take a stand much nearer to the centre of the political spectrum. In one sense, this decision was a logical extension of the modernisation of Labour that had begun under Neil Kinnock and John Smith, a process in which women played a key role. 'Old Labour' had its roots in male-dominated trade unionism and old-style industrial economics. A modernised Labour Party had to adjust to a changing labour market and to the changing roles and aspirations of women, both at home and in the workplace. Crucially, it had to find new ways of appealing to women voters, whose traditional reluctance to support Labour had helped bring about four successive election defeats.

By and large, the women who were active in the Party in the 1980s and 1990s, and who helped to modernise it and extend its appeal, were inclined towards feminism. They supported the idea (for example) that women and men should have an equal voice in parliament and government, and should enjoy equal measures of respect and opportunity in all spheres of life. They campaigned within the party for positive measures to create a more level playing field, and for policies that addressed the specific needs of women as mothers and carers – not to trap them in traditional domesticity, but to enable them to combine paid employment and family responsibilities on an equal footing with men.

New Labour wanted women's votes but was not at all comfortable with feminism – for a range of reasons. Some had to do with the emerging philosophy of the 'third way' and some with a new coalescence of power at the centre of government.

Crucial to New Labour's big tent philosophy has been an ambition to 'level up' (not down). Everyone must be included. Poverty must be eradicated but better-off people must not lose out. Conceivably, economic inequalities may be tackled by 'levelling up' (if only in times of growth). The same cannot be said of gender inequalities. Where women and men are concerned, a great deal depends on how time is deployed - for paid and unpaid labour. Time is a finite commodity. If women are to have real choices in the labour market and the chance to earn an equal living, there needs to be a redistribution of time between women and men. Power, too, is finite. Women cannot increase their political strength unless men give up some of theirs. Equality of opportunity thus requires a redistributive deal between women and men. But that does not chime with an inclusive, loser-free politics.

Inside the big tent there must allegedly be room for tradition as well as modernity. The 'third way' is about 'traditional values in a changed world', prominent among which are *family*, *community* and *responsibility*. According to the Prime Minister, 'reconciling' changes in the role and opportunities of women with 'the strengthening of the family and local communities is among the greatest challenges of contemporary public policy' (Blair, 1998). Under New Labour the family is characterised as a stable marriage where parents supervise homework, prevent truancy, build social capital in the neighbourhood and convey appropriate values to the next generation. This model is not, as routinely implied, gender neutral. Which parent is expected to have time for all those tasks? What chance is there of opportunity in other walks of life for the one who bears the main burden of parental responsibility? Feminism seeks a redistribution of time and power between women and men that would transform relations within the family. As such, it challenges the Blairite proposition that change and tradition can be 'reconciled' without encountering conflicts of interest. No wonder the New Labour leadership prefers to keep feminists out of the tent.

Furthermore, those outside are defined by the size of the tent from which they are excluded. The larger and more inclusive it appears to be, the harder it is to claim legitimacy for dissenting points of view. As New Labour seeks to push out the boundaries, to present itself as neither left nor right, neither liberal nor conservative, but always a bit of both - a synthesis to embrace opposites and end arguments - there is diminishing space in which to acknowledge, let alone address, conflicts of interest or ideology. How can anyone beyond such a far-flung pale be other than a hopelessly incompatible extremist? It follows that insiders are relieved of any obligation to engage with dissent – even when it is essentially loyal and constructive. Either one is in and one buys the whole package, or one is in outer darkness.

And although the tent is supposedly large, its internal arrangements are far from inclusive. New Labour was forged in highly charged, deeply embattled times. It sought to rid itself of associations with the past, tighten discipline and close ranks against adversity on all sides. This has given rise to a closed political culture of elite insiders. In Downing Street's inner sanctum, the occupants are predominantly young, male, white graduates: a generation who grew up feeling that the gender issue was sorted (perhaps by their own mothers) and are inclined to think feminism is yesterday's politics. They enjoy power and do not want to give it up. They have developed a symbiotic relationship with the media, especially the political lobby, which tends to be peopled by similar sorts - men who are complacent about their masculine privileges, who disregard the women's agenda and routinely denigrate feminism. The young men at the political centre can justify distancing themselves from any pro-woman cause on the grounds that this sort of thing always gets a bad press. So the two groups reinforce each other's powers and prejudices.

In the first section of this book, Jane Franklin argues that communitarianism, a favoured perspective of New Labour and the 'third way', has helped to stave off the modernising influence of feminism. Lucy Ward looks back at the public relations disaster of 'Blair's Babes' and asks why all those women MPs, who many hoped would transform the culture of parliament, have so far been unable to assert a shared identity or purpose. Anne Perkins examines the experience of feminist campaigners, walking the tightrope between dissent and loyalty inside the big tent. Melissa Benn considers the relationship between New Labour's 'gender machinery' and women's politics inside and outside the tent. She argues that, ultimately, the fortunes of the Women's Ministers, the Women's Unit and the Equal Opportunities Commission 'depend upon the fate and effectiveness of women in politics as a whole'.

Feminism and democracy

No one should underestimate the importance to women of the policies introduced by New Labour in its first term. Several of the chapters in this volume catalogue the impressive range of measures: the minimum wage, increases in child benefit, new tax credits, the national childcare strategy, new regulations to make working conditions more 'family-friendly and so forth. How is it that, while all this is happening, there is so much unease about New Labour's current stance on women's politics? In trying to capture women's votes while marginalising feminist tendencies in its own ranks, the Blair government has misunderstood both women and feminism.

New Labour's electoral strategy has depended on locating swing voters in key marginal constituencies and finding out what will make them cross the line on polling day. During the 1997 campaign, the phrase 'Worcester Woman' emerged to describe the quintessentially middle-England swing voter who must switch to Labour in order to secure a victory. Worcester Woman was in her thirties with a husband, a mortgage, a job, probably part-time, and one or two children. She was mainly concerned about the economy, schools and health services.

In their quest for Worcester Woman's vote, Blair's strategists could see no common ground between New Labour and feminism. Was their quarry not, at heart, a 'small c' conservative, untroubled by gender politics and probably the last woman in the world to call herself a feminist? Once this calculation was made, the freezing out of feminism could easily be justified.

They had, however, underestimated the extent to which women's lives had changed and how this had altered their ideas and aspirations – so that their support could not be sustained simply by massaging their conservative instincts or appealing to tradition. The fact that most women in Worcester and elsewhere did not identify with feminism could not be construed as antipathy. Feminism is, and has always been, ahead of popular opinion. That is what makes it distinctive. Feminists called for the vote when most women didn't know they wanted it. Now they have won it, most women wouldn't do without it. The same could be said of equal pay and laws against sex discrimination, the right to choose if and when to have children and now, no doubt, having more than 100 women in parliament. Opinion research indicates that women tend to organise their political ideas around a strong sense of fairness. That means they do not like the idea of special privileges for women and they do not want men to be treated unfairly. But nor do they want to be treated unfairly themselves. And the history of women's emancipation suggests that, without feminism, fairness for women can be hard to come by and to sustain. The conflict between 'ordinary women' and feminism is thus more imagined than real.

The strategists also underestimated the extent to which Middle-England voters are fed up with politics and politicians, and failed to recognise the gender dimension of this discontent. Women see politics as a world from which they are largely excluded; they identify it as a masculine rather than feminine culture and are therefore more likely than men to find it alienating and untrustworthy. This tends to make their electoral support even more volatile than men's.

The men in Tony Blair's inner circle sought to by-pass feminism and get straight to those crucial female votes. They made use of strict party discipline to control the handful of assertive women who had made it into their own ranks. No New Labour candidate or MP or adviser could take the side of women against the party leadership without kissing goodbye to her political career. What the men didn't realise was how much they depended on women leaders and activists inside the party to champion the cause of women, to transform the party's image and practice, and to consolidate its appeal to female voters. This was not a job for yes-women but for strong, free-thinking characters with enough courage to buck the trend. Just the sort who tended to have feminist leanings. Just the sort who were not wanted inside the tent. Some were driven out, others bullied into submission. Only in Scotland and Wales did the new democratic institutions give them room to breathe. Few managed to keep their heads above the parapet in Westminster or Whitehall. It was 'business as usual' with men in control and by mid-2000, it was beginning to have a negative effect on female voting intentions.

However, this was not just due to a failure of Blair's inner circle to recognise the value of pro-woman politics. It was also a sign that, by the turn of the century, political feminism was too weak to meet the challenge. It had no organisation and, among the younger generation, no habit of solidarity. The women's movement of the 1970s and early 80s had something of the character of the trade union movement. Although it embodied a fierce critique of male-dominated unions and eschewed many of their forms, it nevertheless borrowed some of their organisational conventions: large gatherings, small regular meetings, a sense of comradeship and mutual commitment ('shoulder to shoulder' and 'united we stand'), pamphlets, marches and linked issue-based campaigns. Remnants of these traditions can be seen now in the environmental and animal rights movements, but not among feminists. As a movement that could lay claim to any kind of organisation, second-wave feminism fizzled out in the 1980s. Younger women had nothing to join. Some wrote books and articles and spoke out on radio and television, but they did so as isolated individuals. Justifiably, they wanted to feel that they owned their own politics and to some it became important to distance themselves from 'Seventies feminism' and, by implication, any kind of 'sisterhood'. The idea of solidarity was not seen as a source of strength, but as a throwback to a by-gone era. At one of the Fawcett seminars where this book was planned, a woman in her late twenties with a passionate commitment to the women's cause remarked that she had never in her life been to a 'women's meeting' until that day.

Feminist organisation will doubtless re-emerge via the Internet. It may become formidable and it probably won't look anything like the women's movement that preceded it. But it has not arrived yet. In the interim, feminism is facing other difficulties. It has not come to terms with the politics of identity and difference and, in particular, with its own white, middle-class heritage. Feminists are fighting a much more complex battle then in the 1970s and 80s, because a lot of the more obvious goals have been reached (such as establishing the principle of equal pay in law), and because, on the face of it, the government is doing a lot for women. However, the gap between women's and men's pay still yawns wide. Women earn 73 per cent of men's average weekly earnings (ONS 1998) and remain pitifully under-represented in most places where power is exercised. They account for only 27 per cent of local councillors – a crucial political training ground - and an even smaller proportion of senior civil servants (Harman 1999, Schneider, 1999).

There is still much to be done. But the women's movement is weak and individual feminist-inclined activists who would otherwise keep up the pressure for change have had their routes to influence cut off and their confidence thoroughly undermined. (The 'Fat Summit' organised by the Ministers for Women in the summer of 2000 was indicative: it drew attention to the dangers of anorexia – an important issue, of course, but a safe one that casts women as victims and wrongdoers, and does not challenge men at all.) In the masculine undergrowth of New Labour, the tactics of passive resistance are skilfully employed. These involve agreeing with the need for equal opportunity, but not doing much about it, secure in the knowledge that little will change, since the men themselves hold the levers of power. Three things might possibly alter these rather discouraging circumstances: a stronger presence of women in local and national governments, and in other places where power is exercised; a renewed women's movement that is innovative, confident and able to operate inside and outside the tent, and a genuine endorsement of women's politics by those at the centre of power.

In the second section of this volume, Deborah Mattinson tracks recent changes in opinion among women voters and finds that New Labour must continue to modernise and feminise if it is to hold on to 'Worcester Woman's' vote. Anne Phillips asks some disturbing questions about why women should be in Parliament. If women are selected as candidates because party members feel it is important to represent the different experiences of women, is it right that, once they are elected, party discipline should take precedence over any defence of women's interests? Yasmin Alibhai-Brown points out that white feminism has long been paralysed by its failure to engage with the politics of Black and Asian women, and argues for a new kind of conversation, across ethnic lines, about identity and difference. Val Feld and Wendy Alexander show how devolution has given women an unprecedented voice in Welsh and Scottish politics. Mary-Ann Stephenson examines the reasons behind the failing quality of local councillors: the problem is not just that there are too few women, but that too few councillors, male or female, are up to the job. For most women, the demands of work and family already weigh too heavily, but if being a councillor became a paid part-time job, it could arguably attract more women and raise standards across the board.

Juggling work and family

A question that has always been at the heart of women's politics is how to find better ways of reconciling the responsibilities of caring and earning. The fact that New Labour's agenda is so heavily focused on paid work has given the question a new salience. The Government's aim is well-known: to get as many people as possible off benefit and into employment, and that includes lone mothers with school-age children and the partners of unemployed men. But the project has been fraught with difficulties, both for the Government and for the women who are targeted by its policies.

As Tony Blair hinted in his Fabian pamphlet (Blair, 1998), the Government's efforts to get women into paid work run awkwardly alongside its espousal of 'traditional' family values, which expect a great deal of time-consuming input from 'parents'. Unless more is done to encourage men to spend serious time on unpaid domestic labour, the required parenting input is bound come from women, who have traditionally regarded it as their prior responsibility. (And for lone mothers, of course, there is no other option.) While this is the case, women cannot develop their earning power or enjoy genuinely equal opportunity in the labour market. Traditional patterns of family life and modern patterns of female employment are not readily compatible.

The Government has introduced a raft of policies to mitigate the problem: the minimum wage, the working families tax credit, and increases in child benefit are designed to make it worthwhile to go out to work rather than depend on benefits, and to boost the income of low-paid workers, most of whom are women. The national childcare strategy, the childcare tax credit and new policies to reduce maximum working hours, to introduce parental leave and to extend new rights to part-time workers are intended to make it easier to combine parenting and paid employment. The Government has also taken significant steps to address the particular difficulties of one-parent families, the great majority of which are headed by women: the New Deal for Lone Parents and the reform of the child support system are aimed at helping lone mothers into paid work once their youngest child is at school, and ensuring that non-resident fathers make a reasonable contribution to the maintenance of their children. The full impact of all these measures had yet to be felt at the time of writing, but they are well intended and undoubtedly a vast improvement on the arrangements inherited from the last government. The difficulty for New Labour lies in holding the line between tradition and modernity, and trying to balance competing claims for equity and choice – an uneasy and unstable combination.

Most women want to work (part-time if not full-time) and this is the only way in which welfare dependency and family poverty can be tackled simultaneously. However, in developing policies to encourage female employment, the Government is vulnerable to claims that it is driving women into the labour market at the expense of the parenting their children need and deserve. At present, women bear the practical burden of that dilemma – trying to do both single-handedly. This makes a nonsense of equality of opportunity between women and men and undermines the income-generating capacity of women throughout the life cycle. Disadvantages accumulate and increasing numbers of women face an impoverished (and consequently less healthy and self-sufficient) old age – which will surely bring heavier claims upon the welfare state. Failure to tackle the problem would thus be inconsistent with two of New Labour's most cherished values: social justice and fiscal prudence.

Three broad approaches are worth considering. The first is to acknowledge that there is economic and social value in caring (both for children and for dependent adults) and to offer some forms of recompense, so that those (mainly women) who use their time for caring more than for earning can enjoy an independent income and perhaps accumulate rights to more than a pittance of a pension. This is consistent with the Government's commitment to 'traditional' family values and to reciprocal rights and responsibilities. But it places new demands on the public purse at a time when the Government is trying to contain spending on state benefits and it could create a new form of 'welfare dependency'. It is consistent with the feminist analysis of the economic value of domestic labour. But it threatens to entrench traditional male and female roles and to close off opportunities for women to compete on equal terms with men in the labour market.

The second approach acknowledges that women's capacity to combine caring and earning to their own satisfaction, and to enjoy equal opportunities at work, depends on men changing their attitudes and behaviour, both in the labour market and in the domestic sphere. It follows that men must be encouraged to be active, caring fathers, and to see this as intrinsic to their identity and their responsibilities. The aim is to ensure that parenting and breadwinning can be shared by women and men on an equal and interchangeable basis. This is consistent with the Government's commitment to social justice and 'opportunity for all'. But it signals a break with tradition and threatens to interfere with the advantages some men currently enjoy on the other side of the glass ceiling. It is also about facilitating social change and may be felt to be uncomfortably *dirigiste*. It is consistent with feminist arguments that equal opportunity at work and freedom of choice cannot be achieved by women unilaterally, but require profound changes in gender roles and identities. It does, however, mean that women must be prepared to share with men the implied rights of the domestic sphere (whether it is access to children or the kitchen, or both) as well as the responsibilities. Following through the logic of this approach is not a soft option. It takes politics on to a more intimate and sensitive terrain than the first approach, where proceeding by consensus (probably the only way in gender politics) is a delicate and highly charged business.

The third strategy is to promote choice. This acknowledges that different work/parenting arrangements suit different family circumstances. It promotes flexible childcare services and working conditions, but does not overtly seek to influence the decisions of women or men, beyond removing constraints as far as possible. It is likely to be attractive to the Government, because it appears to be non-contentious, inclusive and gender neutral. It is consistent with the individualism and commitment to personal freedom that New Labour has embraced on its right flank, and to work well within the 'big tent'. Freedom of choice can be good for everyone, not just for mothers, nor even just for women. The trouble is, however, that the choice option is either very radical and potentially transforming or hopelessly bland and self-defeating. If women who are Black or Asian, who are poor or lone parents or otherwise vulnerable, are to have genuine choices about how they balance work and family, the implications are extremely far-reaching and present a powerful challenge to any government, but especially one that wants to 'level up' and keep its peace with Middle England. If that challenge is not met, then freedoms and choices will simply pile up among those who already have them.

The choice option also has attractions for feminism. It can be construed as non-threatening. It can help keep doubters on board and detractors at bay. Even in its non-radical guise, it may facilitate some progress. But the danger is that it glosses over conflicts of interest (between women and men and different social groups) that must be acknowledged and addressed if feminism is not to renege on its egalitarian ambitions.

These dilemmas will not be resolved easily or swiftly, but they do need to be addressed in open debate inside Blair's big tent. A point to be debated, I would suggest, is that ultimately there may be no just or practical alternative to the radical choice option. Arguably, it has the potential to be inclusive and egalitarian. However, winning broad support for it will require political courage. It won't be achieved by spin or subterfuge, only with a clear head, a stomach for argument, a vision to sustain long-term incremental change, and strong leadership.

In the third section of this book, Stuart White and Diane Gardner examine the meaning of 'civic reciprocity' – that is, how social rights implied in citizenship are balanced by responsibilities to society. They argue that traditional and market based models are out of place in modern social democracy; they call for a new understanding of the value of social care and suggest how obligations may be shared between employers, individuals and the collective resources of the state. Ruth Kelly looks at different models of family life and considers how they are valued by government and how this may be reflected in social and fiscal policies. Harriet Harman examines evidence from recent research into the effects on children and women of different patterns of female employment. She considers the policy implications, sets out proposals for giving mothers and fathers more choice, and recommends structural changes to facilitate 'joined up' social and economic policies for families and children. Matthew Taylor and Alexandra Jones make the case for extending choice to achieve a 'work-life' balance to those without family responsibilities. Only thus, they argue, can a broad alliance be built in support of feminist goals.

Towards a bigger picture

As we head towards a general election and perhaps a second term for New Labour, there is a strong case for giving more room in politics and policy-making to women and to gender politics. A stronger female presence will help to signal to women voters that the party really is changing and becoming one with which they can identify, and one they can more readily trust. It should also improve the chances of including in the party's power-broking and decision-making circles women who are prepared to stand up for the specific needs and interests of other women. (The numbers of men who are prepared to make this a priority are, by all indications, negligible.) But a stronger female presence is not enough. Gender politics must take its place at the heart of policy-making. Gender politics and feminism have different meanings and interpretations, but are closely linked and arguably the former has emerged from the latter. Gender politics is not just about standing up for women. It is about interrogating masculinity and the specifics of male experience, as well as femininity and female experience – acknowledging that gender (as opposed to sex) is constructed, not natural or god-given. Feminists were the first to introduce a critical gendered perspective into 20th century political life. As feminist thought has evolved over the last three decades, the process of opening up to ideas about men and problems associated with masculinity has been part of its own modernisation. This has included a growing certainty that social justice for women cannot be found in simply having more of what men have, but requires a transformation in men's lives too.

A gendered perspective on politics points the way to addressing some of the government's most pressing problems. New Labour is increasingly concerned about young men not taking responsibility for their children, about boys under-achieving at school, about the rising tide of young offenders, who are almost all male, about the failure of young men to get jobs, about older men disabled by work-related illnesses, and about the fact that men suffer disproportionately from heart disease, suicide and premature death. All these factors are rooted – partly or wholly - in the ways in which time, power and responsibility are distributed between women and men, and the subsequent impact on male identities, lifestyles and opportunities. Gendered politics and a redistributive deal between women and men are therefore necessary, not only to achieve a fair deal for women, but also, ultimately, to improve the well-being and life chances of men and women, to maximise human capital and to build a more secure and contented society.

In the final section of this book, Patricia Hewitt demonstrates the need for a gendered perspective on the politics of the 'knowledge economy'. She maintains that, in the new economy, social and economic policies cannot be dealt with separately: childcare, skill building and community development are as much a part of economic policy as managing interest rates and taxation. Liz Kendall and I consider the health policy agenda. We argue that, in order to be relevant and effective, decision-making must take account of the multiple determinants of health and gender, as well as the relationships between them. Policy-makers must contend with social and economic conditions that are changing rapidly, and with traditional structures that are resisting change; both processes – change and resistance – shape and are shaped by gender relations. Ian Christie and Michael Jacobs identify an emerging politics of 'quality of life', with roots in feminism and environmentalism. They suggest that both movements may gain new strength from building alliances at local, national and global levels – and that this may point the way to a new political agenda for the new century.

New Labour needs to acknowledge that gender politics are integral, not marginal to 21st century social democracy. Feminist perspectives will help, not hinder, its ambitions to achieve social justice in a changing world. A one-dimensional 'Third Way', crafted almost exclusively by white males and reflecting their priorities, is intellectually frail and politically vulnerable. If Tony Blair wants to go on leading a modern, electable party, he cannot afford to let his team slide into laddish complacency. The ideas and perspectives that women can bring to the party must be seen not as a set of demands to be mollified by the occasional gesture, but as a key to the continuing process of political renewal.

References

Blair T (1998) *The Third Way* London: Fabian Society.

Harman H (1999) *The Democratic Deficit: A Report on the Under-representation of Women in Local Authorities in Scotland, Wales and England* London: unpublished paper.

Office for National Statistics (1998) *Social Focus on Women and Men* London: Stationery Office, p46.

Schneider R (1999) *Succeeding in the Civil Service: a question of culture* London: cainet Office.

I: The Blair Effect

1. After modernisation: gender, the third way and the new politics[1]

Jane Franklin

There is a dilemma for women in politics today: how sceptical do we need to be about New Labour's agenda for women? Should we hold fire and welcome the slow but significant steps that have been made, or admit to a disappointment and feeling of ambivalence as policies do not quite offer the radical solutions that many women wanted from this government?

One way of understanding this dilemma and the feeling of ambivalence that it evokes is to examine the relationship between feminist politics and the third way. In this chapter, I look first at the influence of feminist ideas on the modernisation of the Labour party in the early 1990s, then at the ideas and principles of the third way which influence social policy. I then ask whether these ideas are compatible with feminist politics. I argue that communitarian ideas, so influential on third way politics, give New Labour the theoretical legitimacy to deradicalise the politics of gender and equality.

New Labour's parallel projects

In their wilderness years, modernisers in the Labour party set out to redesign left of centre politics to fit with the uncertain reality of the post-Thatcher years. Two distinct political positions were to emerge. First, the liberal left, who argued for a socially just, rights based agenda for social policy; and second, those who felt uneasy with individual rights at a time when Thatcher's legacy of the 'me' society hung threateningly in the air. This second group fell upon the communitarian ideas that were exported from the United States and popularised in Britain by the American sociologist Amitai Etzioni and the think-tank Demos (Etzioni, 1993).

Those on the liberal left were influenced by the women who had fought for decades within the Labour party to challenge male dominated politics and to make women's issues a central and defining feature of Labour policy. In conferences, seminars and debates, policies were developed in a dialogue between think tanks, academics, voluntary organisations, local government, politicians and the public, around the key issues where women wanted change. The Institute for Public Policy Research helped to bring these groups together and to develop innovative proposals for family policy (Coote et al, 1990); for child care (Cohen and Fraser, 1991) and for working time (Hewitt, 1993). These policies were based on a liberal left of centre approach which moved beyond the politics of the old left, but held closely to the principles of equality and social justice within a framework of social rights and democratic participation in decision making (Coote (ed) 1992).

In *The Family Way*, for example, the authors recognise that families are a 'social', rather than a 'natural' phenomena, and that more important than the label 'family', is what actually happens within families (Coote *et al*, 1990). They argue that policies should work with the changing patterns of family life rather than impose a model that people cannot and do not always wish to aspire to. The central goal of family policy from this perspective, is that every child should have the right to be dependent and grow up in conditions which enable it to become a dependable adult. It implied a need for 'new responsibilities for men' as well as 'strong and self-reliant women.' Core to this family policy agenda, and subsequently to the policy initiatives of the Commission on Social Justice, is the assumption that men would need to share caring responsibilities in the home so that women could take up opportunities offered to them in the work place (Commission on Social Justice, 1994). There is a recognition in these policy documents of the prevailing inconsistencies in policy making around work and family life and initiatives were developed to change this relationship, so that the incompatibility of working time and caring responsibilities could be recognised and policies developed to reflect the needs and aspirations of men, women and children, at work and at home.

During the early 1990s, women who were central to the modernisation of Labour in opposition worked to negotiate this agenda into the mainstream of political debate. They managed to convince their male colleagues in the party that this was not only a radical and workable political agenda, but that it was what women wanted and would bring them women's votes – which it did.

Meanwhile, a parallel political project was being forged, which challenged many of these left of centre liberal ideas and policies. The search was on for a new political identity, to distance Labour from the now unpopular new right individualism and the welfarist policies of the old left, in order to make it electable. Two questions had to be answered in policy terms: how to build and maintain economic credibility, essential for winning the election and for a place in the global economy; and how to build and maintain a cohesive and settled society, essential for social order and economic efficiency. Key to this project was the need to frame a distinct approach to social policy that would counter the detrimental effects of individualism on society without falling back on an old social democratic position that favoured redistribution and collective welfare provision. The architects of what would become 'New Labour' began to redefine and reframe social democracy to coincide with the needs of a rapidly changing and insecure society. In doing so, they maintained a commitment to social justice and reform, but challenged two basic tenets of social democracy – a commitment to social and economic change and a recognition of the state's role in tackling structural inequality.

New Labour takes a communitarian turn

To redefine social democracy, New Labour took a 'communitarian turn' (Jordan, 1999), switching from the rights based agenda of the liberal left. First, New Labour shifted the goal of social democracy from change to consensus. In the earlier part of the last century, as the Labour party was building its support, social democracy had a radical edge and a political project (Gutmann, 1992). Its goal was change: to work gradually and democratically towards transforming the balance of power and resources in society, between capital and labour, men and women, in the interests of the powerless. The goal of the new social democracy is consensus, to calm down and resettle a society agitated by the individualism of the 1980s. The tacit argument now is that 'old style' social democratic arguments for equality, equal opportunities and social justice, can stir up discontent and political activity which needs to be contained in the interests of social order, within a politics that manages dissent and aims to share the best of what we have in a fair and responsible way.

Second, a political critique of structural inequalities in society has been lost in the shift from the old to the new social democracy. By focusing on people in families and communities and sharing responsibility for social exclusion between different agencies, there has been a tendency to disregard the significance of wider social and economic forces and the inequalities they produce. Indeed, that would be criticized as materialist or 'old' Labour – out of touch with the needs and conditions of the time. People were urged to stop blaming society or global capitalism for their problems and to take responsibility for their own life chances and opportunities and for those of their children. Politicians in today's government, it seems, prefer to shape and harness individual agency and the potential for social change in everyday life, as people make choices about family, relationships and lifestyle that may challenge the traditional social structures and common values that New Labour wants to encourage.

This 'new' social democracy works in harmony with New Labour's liberal approach to economic policy towards a 'third way' that encourages a secure and flexible workforce for a changing and dynamic economy. This co-operative synthesis expresses New Labour's desire to move beyond the oppositional politics of left and right, where social and economic interests were often in conflict, towards a consensus politics where partnership overcomes strife. However, at the same time, it plays down political distinctions and informs an inclusive politics that tends to inhibit opposition and dissent.

Antagonisms between capital and labour, men and women, rich and poor, black and white no longer, in the view of the 'new politics', hold the key to social change. They are acknowledged by New Labour to be an important focus for social policies that encourage partnership and co-operation, but not a basis of political activity or organisation. New distinctions have been identified to supplant the politics of difference in late modern society: inclusion/exclusion, inside/outside; conflict/consensus; safe/unsafe; rights/responsibilities; order/disorder (Beck, 1997). They draw a veil over old configurations that haven't necessarily disappeared and set alternative parameters for decision making. The acceptable choice of consensus, responsibility and cohesion coincides with the communitarian approach, and leads to a framework that is not conducive to social change and can have a dulling effect on political agency.

Communitarianism offers politicians a distinct alternative to liberalism as a guiding approach to social policy. It begins from a 'social' rather than individual perspective, with the idea that people derive their identity, morality and world view from the family or community in which they live. With society as the prime focus, the liberal individual, whose autonomy does not depend on others, is seen by communitarians to bear little or no relation to the reality of everyday life, and has therefore no legitimate basis for politics or policy making. (Mullard and Spicker, 1998) Communitarianism aroused the interest of Labour party modernisers through the work of Amitai Etzioni, who adapted some of its key philosophical principles into a pragmatic set of ideas for policy makers. In his book *The Spirit of Community* (1995), Etzioni describes American society as selfish and greedy, influenced by the detrimental effects of an over reliance on individual rights. He describes a society uncomplicated by economics, power, or the intricacies of class, culture, gender, and ethnicity. These sites of struggle for rights, justice and equality belong, he claims, to an abstract world of liberal principles which have no foundation in people's everyday lives. The only way to bring some certainty and security back to society, is to apply social policies to social disorder.

Communitarianism provides a cohesive framework for policy making, which gives priority to the collective stability of families and communities over individual autonomy. If rights separate individuals from each other and make them greedy and selfish, responsibility binds people together in families and communities and encourages stable and reciprocal relationships. If the universal principles of individual freedom and justice are abstract and have little relevance to people in their everyday lives, communitarians look to inform policy-making with the 'common sense values' that everyone is supposed to understand. The impetus is on building and strengthening moral communities to ensure that fairness and responsibility form the basis of relationships between individuals whatever their class, gender, sexuality or ethnicity. It is 'common sense', in this view, that policies that treat all people equally whether they are men and women, black or white, able or disabled, will lead to a fairer and more equal society. This largely conservative set of ideas donates a political vocabulary and theoretical perspective to the third way, that legitimises a politics seeking to manage and maintain the status quo.

How does the liberal left-of-centre agenda which brought women's interests and a feminist perspective to the centre of policy making in the Labour party fit with this approach? On the surface, family friendly policies that attempt to integrate work and family promise to open up possibilities for women to take up opportunities in the workplace and to encourage men to take on more responsibility for the caring roles at home. They also slide easily into the third way scenario, working to build strong and stable families to provide domestic security to counter insecurity at work. New Labour can keep women on board, reducing the risk of conflict and dissent, while reworking its policies within the communitarian framework. Surely, if they do both, there is nothing to complain about?

In their book, *The Politics of Community* (1993), Elizabeth Fraser and Nicola Lacey help to clarify the complex relationship between feminism and communitarianism. Initially, it is possible to identify shared themes and insights between the two. First, as Fraser and Lacey argue, both perspectives share the notion that abstract and universal categories are largely unhelpful. Feminist theory has long argued that the liberal idea of the individual is essentially male, making women either invisible or seen as 'other' to men. Second, they share the notion that there is no pre-given understanding of social categories (gender, sexuality, family forms) and that individuals take on identities and live in families that have been socially constructed, generated by the community in which they live (Fraser and Lacey, 1993).

Consensus or conflict?

For communitarianism, however, these insights offer the rationale for a conservative, consensual politics, the assumption being that if ways of living arise from the 'natural' order of things, they do so because they work best for all concerned. There is an unchallenged 'common sense' in this view which makes radical political change not only unnecessary, but destabilizing. For feminism, however, these insights only offer a description of the way things are as the basis for a critique of the status quo that demands social change. As Fraser and Lacey point out, communitarianism describes the social basis of women's roles and experience, but this description ends in stasis. It has no capacity for critical analysis and judgement as to whether these social practices are coercive, oppressive or demeaning. There is nothing in the communitarian perspective that allows for the view that there is anything problematic about gender divisions. While feminism may be in tune with a communitarian understanding of the significance of communities in determining the way we live, it is uncomfortable with its approach to politics, since it fails to deliver the critique that it makes possible (Fraser and Lacey, 1993: 138).

Communitarian ideas therefore, work within the third way to diffuse and shape women's politics in at least three ways. First, as an inclusive politics it absorbs radical ideas and diffuses them, making it difficult to focus on women's issues in particular. Second, as a conservative politics it gives consensus priority over change, stressing the destabilizing effect of radical ideas. Third, as a politics of community, it reduces the significance of structural inequalities in society, making change unnecessary.

Etzioni exemplifies the communitarian approach in his concern that individual rights and autonomy encourage women to pay too much attention to their own needs and ambitions, leaving the needs of families and communities unattended (Etzioni, 1993). In fighting for women's rights to autonomy and choice, to a life beyond the front door, feminism, in league with both socialist and liberal politics, has separated women from their families, has made them selfish and has begun a social revolution that damaged community life, now in need of repair. Yet the great advance of the women's movement has been to enable women to stand outside of their everyday experience as wives and mothers, to articulate their needs and interests politically and to find power in a collective identity with other women who have similar experiences. The women's movement has questioned the status quo, it has challenged existing political structures and it has changed them.

If critique is the impetus for social change, then this new politics is out of kilter with feminism, since it chooses consensus and stability over opposition and dissent. Feminism has always been at the vanguard of social change, and has not yet reached the stage in its history when it can afford to be consensual. It is still about 'making waves' (Coote, 1999), about struggle and finding a space to articulate an alternative perspective to the dominant political ideology. It has always been political. So, a set of political ideas that seeks to subdue difference and critique is unlikely to deliver the changes that feminists want.

However, in New Labour circles the prevailing view is that, if we can only see how the interests of women and men coincide, then what is good for one will – by implication – be good for the other. With the focus on how men and women can work together in a partnership for the benefit of each other and especially their children, in work and family life, any suggestion that women have a distinct set of interests and a politics of their own is seen as conflictual. Conflicts of interest have no place in this politics of consent and negotiation and it is unnecessary, in this view, to have a gendered approach to policy-making. For example, the Women's Unit write that:

> The Working Time Directive, which came into force in October 1998, will enable people to balance their work and home lives better by: allowing most people to say that they do not want to work more than 48 hours per week; providing workers with the right to paid holiday every year...all employees should be able to take unpaid leave to cover family emergencies. (Women's Unit, 1998)

This un-gendered paragraph rightly recognises that family friendly policies should enable women to work and that working men are fathers and want to be active parents as well as breadwinners However, policies that treat people the same, whatever their status, tend to hide the influence of structural inequalities and unequal power relationships that remain beneath the surface.

Compare this consensus approach with the liberal left of centre perspective of *The Family Way* (1990) which recognises the different and complex needs and power relationships within families, rather than merely seeing families as a means to a cohesive and ordered society. It acknowledges that the autonomy and rights of individual men, women and children have to be respected to enhance the capacity of families, whatever their form, to raise children to be autonomous and independent adults. It is this individual capacity and confidence that enables adults in families to negotiate equal partnerships in caring and housework which may take generations to build. Imposing responsibilities on people who do not have the capacity to take them on, can cause distress and unhappy family relationships.

Feminism demands equality with men, which inevitably means that men have to give up some of their privileges and power. But New Labour needs women on board, working in the labour market, caring for children and helping to build strong families and strong communities, voting. Of course, women recognise the importance of partnership and consensus, of working with men in politics, in families and at work. Yet they also have a politics that is separate from men: a politics that recognises inequalities and conflictual relationships that cannot yet be addressed with policies designed to favour men and women indiscriminately.

Conclusion

The politics of the third way is a consensual politics. Its social policies promote order and stability in society, and a flexible workforce that a dynamic economy needs it if is to compete in the global market. At the heart of this consensual agenda is a paradox. It seems as though New Labour are working for women, it seems as though they promote equality and social justice through their new social democratic policy framework, but there is a sleight of hand. As Helen Wilkinson has argued, at the same time as women's issues come centre stage in policy making they are, in effect, marginalised (Wilkinson, 1998). A trick easily missed, but possible to detect viewed in the context of communitarianism.

In order to preserve order, the third way needs to absorb troublesome women into the political mainstream. One way of doing this is to subtly alter the shape of feminist arguments for equality at work and at home, to change from a liberal to a communitarian mould, from rights to responsibilities, from conflict to consensus, from autonomous women to women in families. The goal of feminism is change, and though women may find the notion of partnership and negotiation attractive, they are not yet at the stage where this can take place on an equal footing with men, since structural inequalities still exist and still need to be challenged (Phillips, 1999).

Zygmunt Bauman has argued that the stand off between left and right in politics today leaves a feeling of ambivalence (Bauman, 1991:279). This ambivalence is reflected in the dilemma women feel about the extent to which New Labour is working in their interests. It holds back dissent, since it is hoped that things may change and that, with the next election, policies may become more radical. How far can Labour women go down the third way before they can go no further?

Endnote

1   This chapter contains some extracts and ideas from 'What is wrong with New Labour politics?' in *Feminist Review* no 66, Autumn 2000.

References

Bauman, Z (1991) *Modernity and Ambivalence* Polity: Cambridge

Beck, U (1997) *Reinvention of Politics* Polity: Cambridge

Cohen, B and Fraser, N (1991) *Child Care in a Modern Welfare System: towards a new national policy* IPPR: London

Commission on Social Justice (1994) *Social Justice: Strategies for National Renewal* IPPR: London

Coote, A *et al* (1990) *The Family Way: a new approach to policy making* IPPR: London

Coote, A (ed) (1992) *The Welfare of Citizens: developing new social rights* Rivers Oram Press/IPPR: London

Coote, A (1999) 'It's lads on top in Number 10' *The Guardian* 11 May 1999

Etzioni, A (1993) *The Parenting Deficit* Demos: London

Etzioni, A (1995) *The Spirit of Community: Responsibilities and the Communitarian Agenda* Fontana: London

Fraser, E and Lacey, N (1993) *The Politics of Community: a feminist critique of the liberal communitarian debate* Harvester Wheatsheaf: Hemel Hempstead

Gutmann, A (1992) 'Communitarian Critics of Liberalism' in Avineri, S and de-Shalit, A (eds) *Communitarianism and Individualism* Oxford University Press: New York

Hewitt, P (1993) *About Time: the revolution in work and family life* IPPR: London

Jordan, B (1999) *New Politics of Welfare* Sage: London

Mullard, M and Spicker, P (1998) *Social Policy in a Changing Society* Routledge: London

Phillips, A (1999) *Which Equalities Matter* Polity: Cambridge

Wilkinson, H (1998) 'Still the Second Sex' in *Marxism Today* Nov/Dec 1998

Women's Unit (1998) *Delivering for Women: the progress so far* http://www.cabinet-office.gov.uk/womens-unit/1998/delivering/index.htm

2. Learning from the 'Babe' experience: how the finest hour became a fiasco

Lucy Ward

They turned from babes into robotic Stepford Wives, according to one MP. From tarts into nannies, in the words of another observer; sheep into, well, still sheep in the opinion of many more. Never can so (relatively) few politicians have been called so many names over so many newspaper column inches in so brief a time. The story of the so-called 'Blair Babes', New Labour's record-breaking clutch of female MPs swept in at the 1997 general election, is a unique tale of soaring expectations, disappointed dreams and indignant rebuttals, with a few political casualties thrown in along the way. It reveals much about the party which, at first, set so much store by women's election, and about the image-obsessed government Britain elected. And it is a story which, like the New Labour administration, is still unfolding.

The concept of Blair Babes – the name swiftly given by the tabloids to the 101 newly-elected Labour women and, specifically, to the 64 new-intake female MPs – famously begins with a photograph. On 7 May, the first day of term after the election which delivered Labour's landslide victory, the party's female MPs were summoned to Church House, Westminster for a celebratory photocall with newly-annointed prime minister Tony Blair. Smiling jubilantly, many arrayed in the jewel-coloured suits party guidance had advised for campaigning, they clustered eagerly around the leader in a formation some now look back on with embarrassment and regret. 'Blair's babes – the proof that women really have arrived at Westminster,' ran the next day's headline in the *Daily Mail*, which had sent a male correspondent to offer his views on the MPs' outfits. 'I warned No 10 that we would look like sheep and he [Blair] the only ram,' former social security secretary Harriet Harman says now. 'They said I was being prima donna-ish.'

The effect of the photograph, still the touchstone for almost every collective profile of Labour women, was to cast in stone two images of the 101 female MPs: first, that there were, for the first time in history, significant numbers of them (the Tories still dragged their heels with 13, now 14; the Liberal Democrats managed three, now four); and second, that they were loyal, even subservient, to their male leader. For the media, the portrait ('iconic, but a mistake,' according to new-intake MP for Slough Fiona MacTaggart) encapsulated the start of a news story whose unfolding would prove gloomy enough to wipe the smiles off even the most camera-loving faces. Within days, the women's clothes and haircuts were under scrutiny; in the following weeks and months the judgments became tougher still as already-sceptical journalists demanded fulfilment of raised expectations. By the 1000-day anniversary of the Blair administration, passed with little fanfare in January 2000, MacTaggart was spurred to publish a Fabian pamphlet in defence of Labour's women MPs in which she sought to rebut allegations ranging from toadying to ineffectiveness in influencing policy. Three years into government, the media's verdict on Blair's Babes *en masse* is largely of disappointment and dissatisfaction, while the MPs feel misunderstood, hard-done-by and undervalued by prejudiced journalists. But how did such a relationship turn so sour, and is the prevailing view that 'Blair Babes' have had little real impact justified criticism or merely a misogynistic Westminster cliché?

The history of New Labour's influx of new women MPs in fact begins well before the Church House gathering, reaching back some eight years to the early stages of Labour's modernisation. Won over by arguments, presented by women MPs and activists, that the party's electoral recovery would depend partly on establishing female-friendly appeal, leaders Neil Kinnock and John Smith successively introduced reforms including female quotas in the shadow cabinet and women-only candidate shortlists for winnable Westminster seats. The female shortlist system, eventually halted in 1996 after a tribunal challenge, brought 35 new Labour women into the Commons the following year, but left in its wake an often-underestimated degree of resentment. Disappointed male would-be candidates and constituencies forced to accept a women-only list were not the only critics: traditionalist MPs and activists (men and women), who either disapproved of the mechanism on principle or regarded it as an instrument of centralising control by the party's Millbank headquarters, were also discontented.

A bitter battle

Fiona MacTaggart, herself selected via a women-only list, recalls the system's implementation as 'a bitter battle'. The row may have influenced women MPs' media-frustrating preference for consensus over conflict once in the Commons, she argues. 'You must not underestimate the track record a lot of women had in nasty infighting, and the level to which they had been seen as horrible harridans. So it was necessary to recreate ourselves as not horrible harridans in order to do things.' Scarlet MccGwire, a journalist and media consultant who advised many Labour candidates on presentation skills, believes the shortlists were responsible for defining Labour women MPs as 'a homogenous group' and for raising expectations sky-high. 'The problem was, that was not the way they ever saw themelves. MPs are by their nature individual, and there was an inevitable backlash from the women where they wanted to be treated as individuals.' The new-intake female MPs grew increasingly resentful of media coverage which lumped them together and expected collective views, she argues.

But though the seeds of dissent were already taking root within the Labour party, much of the initial coverage of the new Labour women was predominantly upbeat, if occasionally wearying in its focus on the way the MPs balanced home and work lives or the installation of a tights machine in the Commons. Newspapers caught up in the excitement of dramatic political change at first reported more or less at face value the new intake's hopes of a 'culture change' at Westminster and the end of the 'Westminster old boys club'. There were countless newspaper diaries describing early weeks as a parliamentary 'new girl'; glossy magazines profiled the more photogenic 'Blair babes' as they modelled power suits in the shadow of Big Ben. Some reports verged on the breathless: on 5 May the *Mirror* enthused: 'they are young, intelligent, dedicated and strong, and for the first time they are bringing girl power to the mother of parliaments'.

Problems only really set in for the women when their novelty – the prime ingredient of their newsworthiness – wore off and newspapers, already spoiling for a chance to take the shine off New Labour, demanded within months that they justify Tony Blair's boast that they would 'transform the culture of politics'. Even in the drama of the election victory, it had not escaped notice that the promised 'woman's minister of cabinet rank' would not be a full-time post but would be an additional duty for the new social security secretary Harriet Harman. Worse, Joan Ruddock MP was to work as a parliamentary under-secretary for women without a ministerial salary, while in Scotland women's issues came under the umbrella of the unavoidably male minister Henry McLeish. With New Labour's much proclaimed commitment to addressing women's concerns already under question, more critical attention was turned to the new female MPs. Unexpectedly, feminist commentators such as Charlotte Raven, writing in the *Guardian*, were among the first to demand greater substance behind the claims that more women MPs would change the culture and priorities of Westminster. 'Too many of Labour's new intake are feminisers rather than feminists who want to bleat on about crèches without giving these demands any context,' she complained in July, arguing that feminisation had so far meant the conversion of the Commons barber to a unisex salon and the installation of more women's lavatories. Advocates of feminisation were 'like pampered wives who use female wiles when it suits them and cry when they're not taken seriously. They're women when they want to be excused from the boring politics and people when they want to be promoted.' Why, Raven asked, had the new female MPs not demanded a higher floor for the new minimum wage, benefiting hundreds of thousands of low-paid women? 'If New Labour ladies really cared about their sisters, they could have formed a caucus in the Commons and put pressure on the government to do something for women.'

Perhaps more worryingly, individual female MPs began to be singled out for ridicule which was then applied to the new intake women as a whole. The first to encounter such treatment was Helen Brinton, newly elected to the formerly Tory seat of Peterborough and a classic example of the 'unlikely lads and lasses' whom Millbank had never thought to vet thoroughly as candidates. Brinton's key error came during a post-election appearance on Newsnight, when she assured Jeremy Paxman that it was Labour backbenchers' job loyally to follow the leadership line. Within 24 hours, one old Labour male MP was telling lobby journalists, that he was now measuring degrees of new intake sycophancy in 'Brintons' and journalists, from the *Guardian* Diary's Matthew Norman to the tabloid political teams, had found an easy target. Former *Mirror* political editor Kevin Maguire, whose paper had supported all-women shortlists and who readily acknowledges the phenomenon of super-loyal 'Blair boys' as well as babes, recalls: 'Brinton became personified as this new breed of robotic Labour MP. Certainly, on a tabloid, if you tried to argue that not all the women were like that, she would always be the one the newsdesk threw back at you.'

Gradually, despite the fact that all but a handful of the dozens of new intake men remained as invisible as ever, the new women MPs became the symbol of all that was judged worst about New Labour, by journalists and traditionalist MPs alike. Already the product of Millbank manipulation of the selection process, their fuschia suits and low political profiles made them the butt of criticism that New Labour was more about style than substance, about slavish loyalty in the voting lobbies rather than debate. The tone would be summed up in February 1998 when the determinedly off-message MP for Hackney South and Shoreditch, Brian Sedgemore, likened the women to 'Stepford Wives... who have a chip inserted into their brain to keep them on message'.

The benefit bombshell

Amid such generally untargeted insults, one event more than any other shaped the image of the new intake women among sympathisers and enemies alike. On Wednesday December 10, Harriet Harman rose as social security secretary in the Commons to defend one of New Labour's most foolish errors: the decision to abolish the benefit premium for lone parents.

As a 'new-intake' political journalist, just three days into a new job in the Commons, I watched the scene from the press gallery amid a crowd of dissent-starved colleagues. When Blair and Gordon Brown, the chancellor, scuttled out of the chamber after prime minister's questions, Harman was left physically and politically isolated at the despatch box, attempting to defend an indefensible measure which should never have got as far as the Commons, particularly under a government which claims its prime goal is to abolish child poverty. Worse, as the Tories made the most of government embarrassment and old Labour backbenchers spoke out against the cuts, the prime minister was in Number 10 hosting a reception for showbiz stars including Noel Gallagher of Oasis. When, at the end of the evening, all but one of the new intake women (the left-wing and proudly off-message Keighley MP Ann Cryer) voted to support the benefit cut, the picture looked complete: New Labour, fascinated with metropolitan glitz, was ready to junk its pledges to help the poor, and even its much-hyped band of female MPs would not spring to the defence of their sisters.

There was more to the reality, of course, but not much more. All but a handful of new intake Labour men trooped through the aye lobby, and many MPs of both sexes spoke of voting with a heavy heart. In the Budget of the following spring, Brown would take steps to restore the cuts, which were widely claimed to have been a mistake not foreseen by an inexperienced government. Nevertheless, unfair as it seemed to the new women, who still argue that rebellion is a highly serious step which they felt unequipped to take at the time, the media and many voters blamed 'Blair's babes' – and Harman – for betraying their own ideals. What had become of the promises to make sure women's concerns were heard at Westminster? Why had so many either stayed silent or, like Lorna Fitzsimons (MP for Rochdale and chair of Labour's poorly-attended backbench women's group) spoken out in defence of the cuts? Were the new women MPs in reality concerned more with their personal career ambitions than with social justice?

It is true to say that no one put the same charges of disloyalty with such force to male MPs, but then, fairly or unfairly, I believe there were higher hopes of the women. Whether or not they recognised the impact of their words in the first heady days at Westminster, even the most cautious suggestions that parliament and policy would be changed by the influx of women had raised expectations. Today, female political journalists who say they are predisposed to support women in the chamber (we are in an even smaller minority in the Commons press gallery) speak of on-going disappointment springing directly from the lone parents debate. Less favourably disposed commentators, meanwhile, had boosted the women high enough to ensure they fell – and saw them doing so in spectacular style.

For many women observers, there was greatest disappointment in Harriet Harman, who – partly as fall-girl for the lone parent fiasco – lost her cabinet job in the following summer's reshuffle and has since proved a far more effective backbench lobbyist than she ever was a minister. Scarlet MccGwire recalls: 'People said, well, if she can't win on lone parents... And the thing is, she didn't try to win: she thought that was her sacrifice.' Harman now says that, though she has a 'highly developed sense of personal responsibility', the matter was 'a collective error involving Gordon, Alistair [Darling, then chief secretary to the Treasury] and Tony as well as me... But there didn't need to be a good co-ordinated response because they had a scapegoat.'

It is unfair to say the vote permanently damaged the reputation of the women MPs, she insists. 'It absolutely should not have been the body blow that it was. It only was such a blow because they were so vulnerable. Why for example was I more vulnerable than Gordon or Alistair on those cuts? You tend to be more exposed in this kind of crisis if you are a woman.' A 'good political strategy' would have seen the women MPs claiming credit for the huge child benefit increase as a response, she claims.

'They could have hailed that as a victory, and actually that would not have been a misrepresentation of the situation. So they got the blame for the problem but didn't get the credit for sorting it out.'

Harman may have underestimated the impact of the vote, and is, I believe, disingenuous in arguing that she fell simply because she was a woman. Her analysis also overlooks the fact that one effect of the debacle was to prompt the women MPs to spurn any collective identity. Where once they had spoken of the difference so many women could make in parliament, they began to shrug off the 'female MP' tag, insisting that they were as diverse in their interests and talents as their male colleagues. 'There was nowhere to go – the women became individuals,' says MccGwire. The days of promises to 'change the culture' of Westminster had long gone. 'Collective identity meant collective expectations – they rejected that. They would only speak about women in Blairite terms.'

One new intake female MP, angry at the media condemnation which has dogged the 'Blair babes', retorts: 'We are all different: we are not all natural rebels'. A long-time advocate of more women MPs, she nevertheless insists that the realities of Westminster mean the new women MPs could neither have overturned lone parent benefit cuts nor have caused an instant culture change elsewhere. 'We came in as lowly backbenchers – you can't just walk in and expect to run the show. There seemed an expectation that we should storm the palace and run gender up the flagpole. It doesn't work like that... We should be representing our constituents with our perspective and experience. That is why we want more women in: we don't just want suicidal raids.'

Fiona MacTaggart is more willing to admit that the lone parent benefit cut was a mistake, pointing out that it was 'not only foolish but contradictory' since it ran counter to New Labour's policy of making work pay. Unemployed single mothers, faced with the threat of returning to a lower level of benefit if they took a job and then lost it, opted not to look for work – the antithesis of the Brown-Harman policy.

Blanket of silence

But, while acknowledging that the party created expectations of the new women as 'fairy godmothers', MacTaggart argues that six months post-election was 'too early' for them to have gained the experience to oppose the benefit cut before it was imposed. The lesson learned, she believes, is to get your opposition in swiftly and privately, not waiting for high-profile crunch vote to make your views heard. 'It seems to me that the part we are not good at is changing things before they are first written. The most important time in politics is right at the beginning. That is where we have made mistakes.'

MacTaggart can point to instances where behind-the-scenes pressure has had an effect: greater emphasis was placed on family friendly policies as well as trade union reform in the Fairness at Work legislation, and direct representations to home secretary Jack Straw led to changes to the immigration and asylum bill. Women MPs pointed out to Straw that the cost of nappies alone made the derisory level of vouchers for asylum seekers unrealistic, and the sum was subsequently increased. The asylum example, however, illustrates precisely the dangerous bargain that Labour women have bought into – a bargain that means, I believe, that they risk perpetually being written off as a disappointment. It was made clear to the MPs that their private interventions would be listened to, provided they did not make their grievances public. The price of a chance of success was a blanket of silence, a promise not to rock the boat.

When challenged over the implications of this pact, women MPs often claim that they were simply going about the business of politics in a consensual rather than combative way, a 'feminine rather than masculine' approach. Just because journalists want rows, they say, that does not mean that is the most effective means of getting the job done. The trouble with this argument is that, to an excessively image-conscious government such as Blair's, differences only really matter when they are public and, thus, out of control. Ministers might listen to behind-the-scenes pleas, but then they might not, and no one in the media or the country is ever any the wiser that such a case was made and ignored.

The chance of backstage persuasion on issues specifically affecting women is even less under a government which, for all it has created a women's unit, is intrinsically wary of addressing 'women's' concerns, instead banning the f-word (feminism) and preferring to talk of families, rather than women. The women's unit's slogan is 'better for women, better for all', but on issues such as equal pay, better for women may at first mean worse for men – a problem consensus politics cannot duck. 'The women have got to start leaking and arguing,' says one frustrated female journalist. When women MPs do make progress or achieve change, she continues, they should 'really grab the credit: not doing that is one of their worst failings'.

To such pleas for outspokenness, the women MPs can say, with some justice, that they would have been punished by hostile elements of the media as much for 'whingeing' as for toeing the line. One tabloid journalist, who nevertheless says she feels 'personally disappointed at their low impact', agrees: 'If they were too feisty the *Mail* would have hammered them for being trouble-makers; too quiet and it would have accused them of being supine. With the *Mail*, they really couldn't win.'

Jo Gibbons, special adviser to women's minister and leader of the Lords Baroness Jay, says: 'The reason they don't put their heads above the parapet is because, if you are a woman, you get your head blown off far more often than if you are a man. The women are still nervous of speaking out.' She does, however, detect a fight back emerging among some of the women MPs, who are now prepared to stand up for women's achievements rather than reject any suggestion that they be judged as a group. Fiona MacTaggart's research paper charting women's contribution to Labour's first 1,000 days seeks to show that, though women 'have a greater propensity to reject the bold, but doomed, approach of public disagreement', they are 'more likely to persist with the long slow campaign' (MacTaggart, 2000). The efforts of female ministers and backbenchers alike, she argues, have had a distinctive impact on policy, including ensuring the new working families tax credit can be paid to women, improvements to rape law and the lowering of the gay age of consent. 'She is making the case for added value,' says Gibbons, 'saying women brought something to the House that men did not bring.' MacTaggart has also taken the trouble to create links between women MPs and female lobby journalists, though women are still less likely to ring press contacts with stories – or views – than men.

Changing tack

Lorna Fitzsimons, also beginning to forge connections with women in the lobby, is one of the few female MPs to admit a change of approach may be needed. She told me: 'We are very good at doing things in a behind the scenes, non-confrontational way because that is easier and it is less embarrassing. But sometimes, we are recognising, it does not actually work.' Ruth Kelly, the highly able new intake MP for Bolton West, this spring presented a fully researched and costed paper to ministers making the case for turning a new entitlement to parental leave from an unpaid to a paid right: a prime example of the possibility of making a forceful, intelligent and widely-reported argument without apparently losing favour with the party high command.

Harman and Ruddock, too, are fighting energetically from the backbenches: the former social security secretary for improved parental rights and childcare and Ruddock for changes to the Sex Discrimination Act to allow political parties to bring back all-women shortlists. This issue is even said to have won round the prime minister (though any legislation will not come until the next parliament), following pressure from Margaret McDonagh, the Labour Party's first female general secretary.

McDonagh now claims to be a fierce apologist for the women MPs, responding to pleas that they speak out more with a tough defence of their consensual approach. 'We don't want the women to behave more like men: the men have to act more like women,' she says. Critics of New Labour 'control freakery' would take that as evidence that the Labour women are more willingly complicit in oiling the wheels of the party machine, offering easy obedience while men make a fuss. McDonagh argues that 50 per cent of MPs should be female in order to ensure legislation 'reflects the fact that women behave differently', but – despite supporting women-only shortlists – she says the case must be made for women MPs before the law on lists can be changed. Constituency parties are either unconvinced of the case or do not care: by the summer of 2000, only one woman had been selected for a safe Labour seat, prompting suggestions that female candidates will be controversially 'parachuted' into last-minute vacant seats shortly before the next general election.

The difficulty with McDonagh's view is that, as long as female MPs prefer low-profile pressure to public statement, and as long as many reject the premise of judging women as a group, it is difficult to convey to voters what – if any – difference women are making. Yes, much of the media has an agenda to do women down, and Labour's hyping of the Blair Babes made that easier. 'They were always going to get hammered in the tabloids and although the issue is pretty dormant now, I don't think it has gone away,' says Kevin Macguire, now *Guardian* chief reporter. But politics, surely, is nothing if it is not about public statement and visibility. Women are already at a disadvantage in Blair's government: with the exception of international development minister Clare Short, the only female cabinet ministers are in backstage 'fixing' roles with little or no public profile and none of the power that comes from having a budget to spend. Female voters are noticing, and are critical: focus groups conducted by Harman and Deborah Mattinson – director of Opinion Leader Research and an adviser to Labour on appealing to women – found that women thought female ministers had been sidelined and wondered what had become of the change in the nature of politics they had been led to expect.

The same research – published as a Fabian pamphlet in June – powerfully indicated why the government, with an election perhaps only months away, needs to listen to women. It revealed a 'dissatisfaction gap, a 13-point lag indicating women are more disappointed with a lack of government delivery than men (Harman and Mattinson 2000). Such findings, whether female MPs like it or not, hands them collective power, since the government cannot be seen to sideline them, just as newspapers cannot afford to alienate women readers.

McDonagh and MacTaggart are right that women do not have to indulge in rows and posturing in order to make their point (and the days when the media expected Commons rebellions are gone), but that does not mean they cannot make a well-argued, persuasive and above all public case for change, as Ruth Kelly's parental leave paper demonstrated. The media treated her findings seriously, reflecting a dramatic increase in the level of serious, non-mocking coverage of policy issues affecting women in the last year. If it is true, as McDonagh says, that women make policy differently from men, then that differing approach deserves to be seen in the open, in the debating chamber, in speeches, in press conferences and even in conversations with journalists. Where negotiations have taken place behind the scenes, there is nothing wrong with women taking credit for changes achieved: even if they do so individually rather than under a collective 'Labour women' banner. Without such openness, women can have no hope of fulfilling Tony Blair's prophesy that they will 'transform the culture of politics'.

References

MacTaggart F (2000) *Women in Parliament: Their Contribution to Labour's First 1000 Days* Fabian Research Paper, January. London: Fabian Society

Harman H and Mattinson D (2000) *Winning for Women* London: Fabian Society.

3. Campaigning in an era of consensus: must women wear the velvet glove?

Anne Perkins

The room is so packed you can hardly see the gold wallpaper. In one corner, the Chancellor of the Exchequer, listening politely to a group of smartly-dressed women. In another, the Social Security Secretary, with the absent expression of someone who isn't paying as much attention as he ought. There are other government ministers – Scottish Secretary John Reid, Patricia Hollis, Margaret Hodge – circulating among the crowd. Everyone's in suits.

It's open house for women in Downing Street. Today it's No 11 and the Chancellor, entertaining women (and men) who've got back to work through the New Deal for Lone Parents, and the job centre advisers who helped them. But another day it could just as well be mothers and toddlers at No 10 or a charity function elsewhere in the Whitehall village, like the great bash for Womankind Worldwide, hosted by the Lord Chancellor when he was having a rough ride over his interior decoration choices. This is the Third Way in action, government for all of the people, friends with everyone, favours for none.

An administration which believes in progress by consensus, in identifying and delivering policies that will appeal to as many people as possible, for as much of the time as possible, should be an approachable government, a government interested in getting people on board, yet the evidence suggests it makes campaigning in many respects less straightfoward. For it is, famously, a government anxious to the point of obsession about the saleability of policy, however great the support is for specific ideas among individual Cabinet ministers (if in doubt, remember the public agonising over Section 28, the legislation which effectively stopped teachers mentioning homosexuality, whose abolition was favoured by most cabinet ministers). It is a government which by definition has abandoned Labour's traditional client groups and is no more than passingly polite to many of those people who cheered so lustily on 1 May 1997, believing they at last had a government they could call their own.

As a result, women's pressure groups in pursuit of radical change have to make fine judgements about when, and where, and how, to push – and when to compromise or to hold off . They have to consider what this Labour government wants to do rather than what they feel it ought to do, and they have to balance those decisions with their own and their supporters' instincts to fight for everything they believe in. This chapter will look at the impact of the government's desire for consensus on individual campaigns – and the impact, and potential dangers, for campaigners of being drawn into the big tent.

Don't mention the 'F' word

The briefest reflection on what has and hasn't succeeded so far underlines the need for campaigners to consider carefully the government's own framework of objectives. As Blair's first administration passes the half-way mark, the evidence suggests that even where it has accommodated its core vote by addressing traditional Labour issues, it has only done so discreetly. Ministers may listen to all the arguments but they only act on the ones that won't scare *Daily Mail* leader writers. Above all, no-one should make the mistake of thinking that, because there is a Minister for Women and a Women's Unit in the Cabinet Office, that this is a government interested in feminism. The f-word is still the biggest turn off in the corridors of power, regarded as a sectional interest and a scary reminder of Ken Livingstone's GLC (however many of his old mates now work in and around Downing Street) and other past embarrassments. There'll be parades of policies for women at the next election, but no shouting in the mass media about what has been achieved by feminists.

However, an awareness of the limitations has produced some astute campaigning and some spectacular results. Take the development of the National Childcare Strategy. After years of hard work with Labour in oppositon, the Daycare Trust may have been pushing at a partly open door, but their influence on the development of the strategy has been enormous. 'Quite gratifying,' comments the Trust's Director, Collette Kelleher, with monumental understatement. 'We had two objectives. We wanted to get our analysis that childcare was a public issue accepted by government. And secondly, because sharing a critique is crucial, we wanted government to accept our view of what the problem is and what needed to be done about it. And in the White Paper, *Meeting the Childcare Challenge*, it was.'

Professor Ruth Lister is equally pleased at the victory won by the Women's Budget Group in getting the Chancellor to change his mind about how to pay the Working Family's Tax Credit (WFTC). The Treasury was committed to paying it through the earner's pay packet because, it was said, in most families both parents were in the labour market. But where they are not, Ruth Lister argued, it is imperative that the main carer gets the cash. Otherwise it would not reach the children. The campaign succeeded in changing the plan so that it is now a matter of choice which parent is paid the actual cash. 'It's not good enough,' says Lister, 'but they listened, and they consulted, and I think they've seen the light now. If you want money to benefit children, it must go to the caring parent.'

Along with these successes, and many other lower profile ones, such as matching the length of statutory maternity leave and the amount of statutory maternity pay, there have been some big misses. So what do the successes have that other campaigns don't? Why, on the list of failures, for example, do we find the campaign for all-women shortlists for the new Welsh and Scottish parliaments (although its defeat did lead to the successful alternative of twinning) or a national strategy to end violence against women? If you are campaigning with the grain, as the Daycare Trust has been, then there will be an audience anywhere in Whitehall (at least where the Chancellor's remit runs. There are tensions between him and others in Cabinet, such as David Blunkett, who would evidently prefer women to be at home with their pre-school children). For Gordon Brown, the dominant voice in this area of government, childcare is about giving women the opportunity to get back to work and off benefits. It is a key part of the war against poverty and the expanding cost of the welfare state. However much some ministers may regret it, it is only incidentally about giving women more choice and more control over their lives.

For example, Ruth Lister's winning argument over WFTC was that it would be the most effective way of using the cash to tackle poverty among children, not that it was a recognition of the role of women as the main family carers. 'There was absolutely no mileage in saying, "this is a woman's issue"', she says. And what distinguishes it from the other, failed, campaigns is that the latter are pre-eminently about tackling the inequalities which continue to constrict the lives of millions of women. As such, they simply didn't register on the ministerial action-scale. It wasn't that government didn't listen: ministers simply didn't think there was any mileage in taking action, especially when they ran the risk of alienating business, new Labour's key constituent.

'The bits they are not doing'

The barriers hit by the paid parental leave campaign reveal much about the negative way consensus politics operates, especially when practised by your friends. The campaign's main voice is Christine Gowdridge of the Maternity Alliance. 'It's hard not to think you've got it made when one of your founders [Baroness Helene Hayman] is a minister. And we do approve of an awful lot of what they are doing. The cross-departmental stuff is fantastic. But we haven't yet got the technique of saying "thanks, but...." Although we did write to Margaret Beckett when she was at the Department of Trade and Industry just to say thanks for something she'd done, apparently it had never happened before. The problem is the bits they are not doing.' A prime example is the reluctance to introduce parental leave with pay. 'This is where I have real problems', says Gowdridge. 'Leave is useless for most people unless it is paid, and it's shameful to introduce something which is only for the well-paid. How can they argue against it? It has been really painful for a lot of us.'

What makes it harder is the knowledge that the ministers involved accept their argument that parental leave won't be taken up unless money is attached. The recent decision to extend statutory maternity pay so that it covers the same period as statutory maternity leave confirms it. But with the fate of Harriet Harman, the only overtly feminist minister, as a warning of its risks, other ministers keep their campaigning on women's issues low key (although some women backbenchers, infurated by accusations of ineffectiveness in the press, took at one stage to carrying round lists of Labour's achievements for women.) Feminists at Westminster know as surely as, for example, trade unionists that pursuit of a single issue is no way to get up there among the boys managing the Blairite consensus. As far as paid parental leave is concerned, there wasn't room in the big tent for supporters of the idea that the state should spend real money giving real backing as well as official status to the controversial notion of shared parental responsibility.

Christine Gowdridge, with other campaigning ambitions such as improving benefits to young pregnant women who can't work, is cautious not to sound too hectoring now the fight is lost (for the time being at least). 'We can tell them the bits of legislation that need changing, and we can get them changed. We have got very very good relations with civil servants and with some ministers. When we wanted to get the maternity grant from the social fund increased, Harriet Harman said "tell them to double it', so we wrote to Gordon Brown, and he doubled it. They were ready to do more almost than we dared to ask.' (Ironically, the power and influence of Harriet Harman, out of as well as in office and especially with the Treasury, is a constant theme across women's campaigning organisations.)

Despite their success in raising the profile of the issue in the media, despite the access and the good relations, round one on paid parental leave failed. 'We will just go on insisting that it must be paid. And we will use any opportunity to say it,' Gowdridge insists. The problem they believe is not the Treasury, but Downing Street, where antennae quiver nervously at the faintest whiff of hostility from new Labour's new best friends in business. Efforts by Gowdridge and the campaign to head off resistance by direct approaches to the CBI and the Institute of Directors have so far got nowhere. And if business won't buy it, then nor will the newspapers (not known for their own family-friendly working arrangements). A radical administration would defend what it believed to be right. But this is a government that marches under a banner inscribed with the pragmatist's motto: 'Politics is the art of the possible'. For these people, keeping the players inside the tent matters more.

Collette Kelleher at the Daycare Trust is also pondering the next step in the campaign to make childcare available for everyone. 'Making childcare a national issue is *de facto* a public spending issue. The Treasury has been an open door for us from day one, maybe because of Harriet Harman's influence. We've been consulted, asked for advice by civil servants, special advisers and ministers. I think Gordon Brown is definitely more feminist in his analysis than David Blunkett [at the Department for Education and Employment] or Tony Blair who's worried about middle England, where many of the women who can stay at home, do. I think there's a real fear in Downing Street of alienating one group of women by supporting another. It places a great responsibility on us to find ways of listening and keeping in touch with what's happening on the ground.'

Biting back criticism

Kelleher's next target is better childcare for students. 'Students won't get the childcare tax credit, and it's particularly important for mothers who want to skill up before going back to work. At the moment, provision is up to individual colleges.' Talk to Kelleher for any length of time though, and it becomes clear that, passionate as she is about childcare, she believes it has limits as a tool to help women lift themselves out of poverty, particularly in areas where everyone is poor, like parts of the London borough of Harringey where she lives. 'There's nothing but state provision, and it's nowhere near enough. A few hours a day a couple of times a week is not going to break the cycle of deprivation. Women there have no choices.' Privately, she has some sympathy for the Child Poverty Action Group's continuing argument that the benefits system remains the best weapon against poverty. But she also believes that there is no mileage at all in arguing the toss with the government, or of trying to exploit the tensions she is aware of within Cabinet about the emphasis on work as the salvation for poor mothers. Instead she operates by subtle flattery, wooing ministers by inviting them to feel-good public launches which recognise the government's role in achieving the Daycare Trust's ambitions.

Ruth Lister too reports biting back criticism. 'Tactically, it was quite difficult to know whether to carry on fighting [for the WFTC to be paid to the main carer]. If you are too oppositional, you will be cast into the outer darkness. But then again, are you just being co-opted by them? There is a place for the out-and-out oppositional. But if you are, and if you don't give credit where it's due, they won't listen to you.' That appears to be the fate of campaigners from outside the mainstream. The Crossroads Women's Centre, for example, report negative results from their attempts to reach ministers with campaigns such as Legal Action for Women's on the impact of the Child Support Agency on women with violent partners. 'We see civil servants,' reports Ruth Hall of Women Against Rape, whose campaigning issues include trying to get the use of women's sexual history banned in rape cases. 'It's not difficult to get through to them. We have taken part in consultation exercises. But what's the point in consulting us if they go ahead with what they were originally proposing?' The Home Office's claim that it has ended one painful anomaly by removing a defendant's right to cross-examine their victim in courts is dismissed. 'The government uses this change to make it look as if it's doing something. In fact, it's talking about downgrading date rape as a solution to the massive increase in reported rape – when most rapes are by husbands, boyfriends, fathers or dates.'

Among these women, there's an equal sense of outrage that, despite the Women's Unit and a Women's Minister and the claim that all policy initiatives are "gender-proofed" the government has, for example, still introduced the Immigration and Asylum Act, which will leave women and children – as well as men – virtually without cash and send them out into strange towns without the support of other members of their community. Women backbench MPs, such as Fiona MacTaggart and Oona King, tried (privately) to change ministers' minds and won some minor concessions. Cristel Amiss, of the Black Women's Rape Action Project, argues: 'The reality is the increasing vulnerability of women. We know when this kind of legislation goes through, the racists are given a signal. And being without cash and sent to cities not used to refugees and immigrants means women will become targets for racists.' What about acknowledging that the government has done some good? 'That can't even be a starting point for a group like ours. We have to be entirely independent of everyone. Our points of reference are the women who need us. Working with the government doesn't get us anywhere.'

These are policies that have also been questioned much closer to government, by the newly-invigorated (again, thanks to Harriet Harman) Women's National Commission, the government-funded umbrella group of over 200 women's organisations, ranging from the Mother's Union to Stonewall. Its new boss, Christine Crawley, former MEP and now a Blair peer, is merely reflecting the views of her membership when she says women remain deeply concerned about violence against women, the plight of refugees and poverty. 'If the government is committed to consult, we can make consultation valuable,' she says confidently. 'Our role is to interpret the weight and intensity of what we're hearing, and "cock the government's ear" to women's authentic concerns.' But can the WNC succeed where all else has failed, and make this a feminist government? 'If you want to influence government, the case has to be properly made. It's not a feminist agenda, but if you're liberating women from work-life pressures then that is feminism. It's a liberation agenda.'

Who will be Barbara Castle?

It is more than twenty years since Labour last made real strides in adjusting the balance of power between women and men. Equal pay legislation in 1970 and the introduction of Child Benefit in 1976 both involved imposing the recognition of the value of women at work and in the home on their male colleagues and husbands. Both were expensive to introduce in difficult economic times. Although Equal Pay was a TUC cause practically from its foundation, individual unions and many union members bitterly opposed it because it would reduce the value of their work. There was little political energy behind the campaign. But it had crept into the Labour manifesto and from that basis Barbara Castle – a minister who positively disliked being identified with 'women's issues' – was able to take it up as Employment and Productivity Secretary in the late 1960s. Although her motivation was justice and equality and, ultimately, a desperate search for something she and the TUC could agree on after the battles over trade union reform, she was able to get it on to the statute book as almost the final act of Harold Wilson's 1966 – 70 administration.

Back in government five years later, she fought an even harder battle for a new Child Benefit, to be paid to all mothers from the birth of their first child, which would replace family allowances received as tax breaks through the (usually male) pay packet. In eerie echoes of contemporary battles, trade unionists opposed it because it meant less take-home pay, while Castle herself defended it vehemently as the only effective way of helping the poorest families who didn't pay tax in the first place. The importance of Castle's personal commitment is simply demonstrated: her successor, David Ennals, immediately delayed its introduction. And, in the face of Prime Ministerial opposition too, it would probably have died altogether had it not been for a backbench rebellion towards the end of the last Labour government, led by Castle (after she had been sacked by Jim Callaghan) and Joan Lestor.

No government lightly changes the power structures on which it rests. The Wilson administrations leant heavily on male-dominated unions, to many of whose members the Castle reforms were anathema. She succeeded because the party (and the TUC) had already been pursuaded that Equal Pay and a reform of family allowances were desirable objectives. Although their support was more nominal than heartfelt, it gave her the locus to push for their implementation in a Cabinet which could not see their relevance and which was almost overwhelmed by economic crisis. But they also suited her own political objectives – whether it was the short-term political imperative of improving her relations with the unions, or the longer term strategic objective of tackling poverty. She had the drive and the authority to push them through, but crucially she also had enough support among backbenchers in the Commons to convince first Wilson and his Chancellor Roy Jenkins, and then Jim Callaghan, that allowing the reforms to fall would be a worse option than offending the male-dominated trade union rank and file.

The first Blair administration is strongly driven by the need to be different from all previous Labour governments. A desire for fiscal rectitude, inclusivity and competence are the real motivating forces. But there are already signs that in the second part of its first term, and almost certainly in a second term, ministers will be looking for symbols of radicalism which, like Equal Pay and Child Benefit, appease their traditional supporters while being sufficiently mainstream not to alarm the majority of the audience in the Big Tent. Of the simmering issues on the feminist agenda, paid parental leave would be the biggest step since equal pay legislation towards redistributing responsibility in the family. It would be a huge recognition of one of the government's often restated themes, that fathers as well as mothers must share the responsibilities of fertility. If the government disarmed business hostility with a commitment to underwrite the cost, as it does with statutory maternity pay, it could become such a radical symbol. What is less clear, in the current climate, is who would be its Barbara Castle, and press its claims at court.

4. Short march through the institutions: reflections on New Labour's gender machinery

Melissa Benn

Government ministers are fond of reciting the long list of initiatives they have introduced which benefit women – the National Child Care strategy, the New Deal for Lone Parents, improved financial advice to women starting up small businesses and so on. In addition, they point to the existence, for the first time ever in government, of a Minister for Women, with cabinet status, and a Women's Unit, charged since 1997 with making sure that women's concerns remain central to all government policy. Outside government, but still totally funded by it, is the Equal Opportunities Commission whose sole purpose since 1975 has been, through research, legal action and campaigns, to promote the cause of sex equality.

This all looks impressive. But how do we asssess the success – or otherwise – of these new and old institutions under New Labour? Should we, in this apparently post ideological age, be persuaded by the logo of the Women's Unit, that 'better for women is better for all' ?, that we have, in effect, moved to an age of gender, rather than specifically women's, issues? Or do we judge these bodies by an older, fiercer tradition – that is by their preparedness to uphold women's needs and demands, even when these are antagonistic to men's? And, given their entire financial dependence on government, how much should we expect any of them to differ from, rather than defer to, their political masters on a range of issues from women's representation in public life to the needs of the modern family?

The Women's Unit is still a a virgin institution and it is hard, even now, to judge its effect on politics and public life. But it is fair to say that its first two years were pretty disastrous in terms of public relations. Harriet Harman might have been the first ever Minister for Women with cabinet rank but the fact that she also held another major office, as Secretary of State for Social Security, suggested that the 'women's job' came as a kind of add-on. Joan Ruddock's decision to perform the role of Harman's deputy without payment sent out a strange, contradictory message about the importance, or otherwise, of women's work. Then came the sacking of Harman and Ruddock and Harman's replacement by Baroness Jay, who almost instantly proclaimed herself to be 'not a feminist' . If this wasn't discouraging enough, Jay to had a demanding day job as Leader of the House of Lords at a particularly crucial time in the history of its reform.

It was hardly suprising, then, that some political writers, even those supportive of the aims of the Unit, were downbeat, even dismissive, about the chances of the Ministry. The Unit, it was claimed, was tucked away, hidden from the centre of government although there was no geographical, as opposed to political, evidence for this claim: from 1998, it was based at the Cabinet Office. More pertinently, the Unit was compared unfavourably with its brother body, the Social Exclusion Unit, which seemed to attract high level government backing whatever it did. 'There is a suspicion that No 10 is simply waiting for the [women's] unit to wither away from neglect' (Perkins, 1999).

Savaged voices

A further public relations disaster befell the Unit with the publication of *Voices*, the results of a lengthy consultation with women around the country. (Women's Unit, 1999) The 'Listening to Women' roadshow was a continuation of an exercise begun while Labour was in opposition, by Tessa Jowell, then shadow Minister for Women (Jowell was appointed as Jay's deputy in 1998). Large meetings were held around the country in late 1998 and early 1999. There was also a postcard campaign and specially commissioned opinion polls. From the government's point of view, this consultation was designed to find out what 'women' really wanted from it. Consultations inevitably raise the charge of innocence or cynicism. Certainly, a substantial body of popular and academic work already existed which might have informed New Labour of what women really want, such as a better work/family balance, an end to unequal pay, firmer action against domestic violence and so on. There is also the thorny problem that has beset any feminist or women-related enterprise for decades: one talks of 'women' but which women is one talking about?

For all these reasons, *Voices*, the glossy magazine-format publication which showcased the results of the nationwide consultation, was savaged in the press or at least by the women columnists who are inevitably set loose on such initiatives. 'Bland beyond satire', thundered Melanie Phillips 'After taking thousands of soundings from the nation's females, the government's Women's Unit has concluded that they find it difficult to strike a balance between home and work. Well, golly gosh.' (Phillips 1999) 'The report is well intentioned,' said Suzanne Moore in the *Mail on Sunday*, ' but there is something fundamentally wrong with treating women as as exotic minority rather than a diverse majority' (Moore, 1999). In the *Sunday Express*, Aminatta Forna argued that that the document revealed only 'one problem: the nation's women didn't speak with one voice' (Forna, 1999).

Voices is, in truth, a touching and impressive document on a diverse range of issues from health to transport, safety to education. Bland? Possibly, but it reveals a deep hunger and need among women around the country, some thirty years after the advent of second wave feminism, to be listened to with attention and respect. Its real difficulty however is that it speaks of, and to, women, at the same time. While faithfully transcribing many women's comments and wishes, *Voices*, like so many goverment publications, never misses a chance to describe and promote government policy on each issue under discussion. This gives it both a surreal and smug feel. You want better opportunities to work? Here's what the New Deal for Lone Parents is doing for you... You want better health care? We're investing billions in health services over the next few years... One can see in it a metaphor for New Labour's general inability to leave space for dialogue, for real political discussion.

But *Voices,* with its populist pretensions, is actually untypical of the Women's Unit , much of whose work has been of a quite different timbre. *Living without Fear*, jointly published with the Home Office, is a lengthy, considered document on the work that is being done around the country to help women who are at risk of domestic violence. The Unit has also produced studies of all-women citizens juries (White, Lewis and Elam, 1999), published a large scale consultation with teenagers (Women's Unit, 2000) and is currently working on ways to hook women up to Information and Communicaton Technologies.

One of its most original and substantial publications, published earlier this year, *Women's Incomes over the Lifetime,* looks at the long term barriers to equality of pay. It examines in detail both the female forfeit, the ways that women earn less than men before children, and the penalties of motherhood. Innovative, precise and full of concrete examples, the report has commanded widespread attention and respect, its findings picked up by the tabloids and broadsheets alike (Rake, 2000). The Women's Unit's ability to attract substantive, even sensationalist headlines, was also confirmed by its 'body image summit' in June 2000, a public discussion of the destructive effects of the 'superwaif' culture, particularly on young women. The government's decision to ask the Broadcasting Standards Commission to monitor the size and shape of women on television was inevitably denounced as 'political correctness gone wild.' (Leapman, 2000.)

Nevertheless, there remains a core political dilemma for the Ministers and the Unit. While much of its work involves thoughtful and careful attention to the independent needs of women, ultimately it is there to serve and support a government which may in a larger, more ordinarily political sense, be acting against women's interests or simply not moving very fast at all. This, of course, was the observation by critics when Labour abolished the lone parent premium in December 1997: how could a Minister for Women argue for 'women' on the one hand while the same Minister, in another guise, advocated abolition of a small but crucial element of women's income?

The gap between 'official' and 'real' politics was gaping. A similar observation might be made about the role women play in government in general. While New Labour has a reasonable record on appointing talented women to the middle and even senior ranks of government, it remains clear to political journalists and feminist critics alike that New Labour is run by a small circle of elite insider men who make the crucial decisions about policy and priorities (Coote, 1999; Wilkinson, 1998). The decision to abandon women only short lists, one of the few really successful political mechanisms for bringing women into politics in substantial numbers, suggests that there could be far fewer women in Parliament after the next election.

A deeper problem

Obvious contradictions apart, there is a deeper problem for New Labour in relation to the modern woman and the family. To be fair, the government here shares a lack of clarity with society as a whole, but Blairism, a politics that depends so heavily on what it thinks the public wants, has become paralysed: it cannot decide what its core message on, and to, women really is or should be.

Part of New Labour's electoral sucess is built on its apparent ability to tap into the modern and the traditional at the same time . The Blair family itself plays an important part in this image. Cherie Blair has an impressive legal career but the Blair family appears, in all other respects, completely 'normal', in that it is run on traditional gender lines (Benn, 1999). There has, then, been something for everyone in the Blair/Booth household, feminists and traditionalists alike. But is there room for a critique of the family when it is relied upon so heavily for so many political purposes? While the findings of its own Women's Unit research provides empirical evidence of the subtle and cyclical discrimination against women and mothers, New Labour cannot deploy this information to any useful political ends. One can perhaps overplay the Middle England theme, but there is no doubt that Blairism is, at heart, about preserving society's institutions not dismantling them. In this sense there is a profound difference between modernisation and radicalism. Modernisation can incorporate the idea of women being economically active, even powerful. Radicalism requires the re-ordering of the family and associated institutions – politics, business – in order to allow greater justice to exist between its members.

Here, the old feminist messages still have some power: the family remains a site of injustice and inequality, tensions and power struggle. Women lose substantial earnings over a lifetime as a result of their family responsibilities. They also take on the larger share of unpaid labour in the home which both inhibits their 'outside' potential and exhausts them. In addition, they bear a disproportionate responsibility for the famed 'community' with which Blairism has had a long and largely abstract romance. Indeed, one view is that the slow handclapping of the Prime Minister by the Women's Institutes in June 2000 signalled a resentment that ordinary and older women feel at society's neglect of their part in the shadow world of domestic and neighbourhood politics (Coward, 2000).

But New Labour really has no coherent or passionate public position on these questions. Domestic violence apart, the government is simply unwilling to concede that any tension exists between men and women, mothers and fathers, in relation to children, work, time, leisure or indeed politics. It talks about everything from parenting to promotion in entirely gender neutral terms, while its Women's Unit works away at the sidelines analysing the very deep and subtle reasons why these experiences are anything but gender-neutral. New Labour may, to some audiences, acknowledge the very real difficulties facing women in contemporary life, but it still pushes an almost wholly traditional message from its political centre. There have been some welcome minor reforms on the work/life balance – the introduction of parental leave, albeit unpaid, and a review is pending of maternity benefit and paternity leave, as well as many fine words to business on the need to help workers find a better balance. However there is little sense conveyed that these issues may or should apply to men as much as to women; that a just family life requires fathers to work less if mothers are to work more, or simply to have some free time! Nor has there, yet, been a robust challenge to business on the well established problem of the long-hours culture that is destroying the quality of so many lives. Modern yes, radical no.

Opportunity knocked

Similar confusions inevitably haunt the work of the Equal Opportunities Commission which, for the first time in nearly two decades, is working with a government not actively hostile to its existence. Unlike the Women's Unit, the EOC is semi-independent from government with a wide range of powers including the right to pursue formal investigations of sex discrimination, to help individuals bringing claims under the Equal Pay and Sex Discrimination Acts, to commission and undertake individual research and to make proposals for policy change to government. The EOC once promised great things. As Polly Toybee has observed, 'In its bright new dawn at the close of 1975, it looked set to become a huge engine for change. As a Commission, it has legal powers. It has governmental authority and status. It has a big budget. When it speaks, the nation should listen' (Toynbee, 1993). However, it has exercised these powers with mixed success over the years. It has pursued some crucial legal cases, particularly, in recent years, on equal pay for work of equal value. But as a campaigning body it has had less success and has rarely posed a robust or strategic challenge to government. Ironically, the most radical period in the EOC's history was during the Thatcher years when its Chair was Joanna Foster, a former head of the press office at Conservative Central Office. The EOC backed the controversial case of Deputy Chief Constable Alison Halford, who claimed sex discrimination against the police force and vigorously opposed the Government's decision to opt out of the Social Chapter at Maastricht, with all its implications for women's pay and employment status. In contrast, the EOC under Kamlesh Bahl, appointed at the tail end of the Major govenment, kept a low profile.

To some extent, the EOC must re-invent itself under each political administration.

What are the tasks for such a body under the benign if rather bland wing of New Labour? So far, it looks as if the EOC will take a softly softly approach. New Chair Julie Mellor is a working mother with a background in business, working part time in her role. There has been extensive internal reorganisation, under new Chief Executive Lynn Berry, and a re-focussing of EOC priorities and public work. The EOC is currently concentrating its resources on its 'Valuing Women' campaign, an attempt, in their words to 'raise public and business awareness of the pay gap and the benefits in getting rid of it' (EOC 2000). The emphasis of the campaign is on getting businesses themselves to monitor and remove their own pay inequalities through 'transparent' pay systems and regular pay reviews. With the TUC, the EOC continues to lobby the government on long overdue reform of the Equal Pay and Sex Discrimination Acts. It is impossible to know how effective this largely voluntary approach will be. The EOC is urging the government to be 'bold' in its approach to this and other issues, such as maternity benefit and parental leave. But how far can and will it push the government when reform is too slow? Radicals argue that the EOC should use its campaigning capacity more effectively to pressure the government and deploy its legal powers to press particular companies to act, as well as continue to take legal cases of strategic importance. In this respect, it is significant that the recent case challenging the government on its refusal to backdate the right to parental leave was taken up not by the EOC but the TUC.

The EOC is wholly funded by government and cannot risk too much boldness itself for fear of getting budgets cut. But critics of its historic caution point out the achievements of its sibling body, the Commission for Racial Equality under Sir Herman Ouseley, its Chair until early 2000. In recent years the CRE has mounted a strong and highly controversial advertising campaign against racist stereotypes and a hugely popular campaign against racism in football called 'Kick it Out'. It has also tackled racism in the Army, one of Britain's most traditional and conservative institutions. Sooner rather than later, the EOC will have to decide whether co-operation with business and polite lobbying of Ministers is enough. Imagine the public impact if, rather than leaving it to business to regulate itself, the EOC chose to investigate the pay systems of a large private company- say, a national newspaper? The effect could be explosive, and would leave no company certain that it could avoid public scrutiny of its age old discriminatory practices.

But the frustrating paradox for bodies like the EOC and the Women's Unit is that, ultimately, their power, or lack of power, does not lie with them. There may well be a Fabian-style influence that strong women within government can exercise on individual Ministers or government policy as a whole, be it Fiona Reynolds, the respected head of the Women's Unit or Baroness Jay, who has come to be seen as a surprisingly effective political player. As diaries and biographies show, this is often how 'real' government works. In early 1998, for example, a number of Labour women MPs told me, strictly off the record, how the debacle over the cut to the lone parent premium in December 1997 had directly led to the Spring budget of early 1998, which put child care and the problem of child poverty at its centre. A political lesson had been learned, even if it was not acknowledged in public. Ultimately the fate and effectiveness of the Women's Ministers, the Women's Unit and, to some extent, the EOC depends on the fate and effectiveness of women in politics as a whole. It needs the continued presence of a 'critical mass' of women MPs, Ministers and sympathetic civil servants to keep the pressure up, to continue to communicate the 'voices' of women in the country through official and unofficial political channels. It will also require individual women to have the temerity to argue for radical changes, and so reject the Blairite consensus that ' better for women is better for all'. Some policy changes may be better simply for women. Under New Labour, it takes a brave woman to do this. Being a feminist has never been a smart career move, and I doubt that it ever will.

References

Benn M (1999) 'Party Impressions' in *Madonna and Child: Towards a New Politics of Motherhood* London: Vintage.

Coote A (1999) 'It's lads on top in Number 10' *The Guardian* 11 May

Coward R (2000) 'Has Labour lost its touch?' *Observer* 11 June

EOC (2000) *Valuing Women* http://www.eoc.org.uk

Forna A (1999) 'Scrap this Seventies feminist throwback' *Sunday Express* 10 October.

Leapman B (2000) 'Farce of TV weight Watch' *Evening Standard* 21 June.

Moore S (1999) 'How dare these Labour ladies patronise women' *Mail on Sunday* 10 October.

Perkins A (1999) 'Women: Take Two' *Guardian* 1 June

Phillips M (1999) 'Women want the right to work – and not to work' *Sunday Times* 10 October.

Rake K (ed) (2000) *Women's Incomes over the Lifetime – Explaining the Female Forfeit* London: Women's Unit, Cabinet Office

Toynbee P (1993) 'RIP:EOC' *Guardian* 23 August

White C, Lewis J and Elam G (1999) *Citizens' Juries: An Appraisal of their Role Based on the Conduct of Two Women Only Juries* London: Women's Unit, Cabinet Office.

Wilkinson H (1998) 'The day I fell out of love with Blair' *New Statesman* 7 August 1998, p9-10

Women's Unit (1999) *Voices* London: Cabinet Office.

Women's Unit & Home Office (1999) *Living Without Fear – An Integrated Approach to Tackling Violence Against Women* London: Cabinet Office

II: Closing the gap in democracy

5. Worcester woman's unfinished revolution: what is needed to woo women voters?

Deborah Mattinson

The media made much of the notion of 'Worcester Woman' before the 1997 General Election. This mythical creature was the 'Middle England' female floating voter deemed to be critical to electoral success. This chapter explores how women's votes do matter, examines what happened in 1997, and, using recent focus group evidence suggests a way forward for politicians wishing to woo women voters in the future.

History of the gender gap

If the Suffragettes had not succeeded, and women had never had the vote, Labour would have won every General Election since the Second World War, or so the story goes. In fact, the apocryphal tale is inaccurate – Labour did badly among both men and women in the 1980s. It would be, however, true to say that if only women had ever voted 1997 would have been the first General Election won by Labour

Certainly, there is no doubt that the so-called 'gender gap' – the Conservative percentage electoral lead over Labour amongst women, less the Conservative lead over Labour amongst men – has dogged the Labour Party through several decades. At its peak in the 1970s it soared to a massive 12 per cent. It closed briefly in the late 1980s, largely due to Labour successfully appealing to younger women voters in the run up to the 1987 General Election. However, it reappeared in 1992 at six per cent, and, even in 1997, still existed although at the much lower level of two per cent.

The qualitative research evidence is still more stark. Up until the mid 1990s, women really did see the main parties differently with Labour characterised as being 'male', 'old fashioned' and 'working class'. The party was seen to be both *for* and *of* traditional working men and at best did not share any common values or aspirations with target women voters and at worst cast Labour in a very negative light. For example, one woman voter in 1992 said that if the Labour Party were a person, 'it would be an old man in a cloth cap with a pipe and a pint'. Another speculated that it would be 'very aggressive, maybe drunk, shouting all the time'.

By contrast, the Conservative Party, was, in essence, more female, not least because for much of this time, it was actually headed by a woman.

> We all loved Maggie didn't we? She was sort of on our wavelength. (Woman voter, 1992)

> When Thatcher was in a lot of women, especially older women, related to her a lot. They wouldn't hear a bad word against her. (Women voter, 1999)

A different view of politics

To understand the roots of these attitudes, our starting point must be a better understanding of the women themselves, whose whole approach to politics and government differs fundamentally from that of their male counterparts.

Traditionally, women have taken much less interest in large 'p' politics. In the early eighties it could be very hard to recruit women respondents to focus groups if the topic for discussion was revealed in advance as being politics. Researchers sometimes deployed tactics of subterfuge to encourage attendance suggesting that the group discussion would cover 'everyday issues affecting all our lives' One participant commented

> When I was asked along here, she said it would be about everyday things.
> If I'd known it was about politics I'd have said 'take my husband he's got
> the time to think about all that – I haven't! (Woman voter, 1986)

Politics has often been seen as a male game; as a luxury that many women have not had time for, busy as they are with their multiple tasks of running a household, looking after children or grandchildren, and, increasingly combining these activities with paid employment

> Men have more time to think about politics because they don't do everyday
> running of the house.

> Men tend to only be worried about one thing – their work – so they can fit
> in the time to think about politics, too. We're juggling much more – two or
> three jobs at a time – and we don't have the space.

> (Women voters, 1999)

Politics has been felt to be irrelevant to women's lives – a talking shop that bears no relationship to the compelling issues of everyday life. Women also believe themselves to be more responsible, caring and dutiful than men. This may have meant that, historically, they would be less suited to the traditional model of how politics works

> I think that they (men) study things like the interest rate and financial things
> more, while we look at things like education and health – the sort of things
> that affect us directly.

> We are less aggressive and more caring.

We take on responsibility without thinking about it, whereas they want a medal if they do the littlest thing.

In politics you have to be out for yourself and that's more like men are.

(Women voters 1993/4)

What happened in 1997?

In 1997, the gender gap did not close. However, the net difference between men's and women's votes shrank to around two per cent, with Labour attracting more women's votes across all ages than it had done for years, and finally getting through to the group that had been most difficult to shift: the over 55s.

Again, qualitative research evidence is helpful in illustrating what lies behind this data. Women observing New Labour developing in the run up to the 1997 General Election believed that they were witnessing the start of a new approach to politics. They saw a political party that seemed to recognise how their lives had changed, and responded to that change.

It was twenty years of Thatcherism and in twenty years things have changed. When I had my daughter it wasn't a normal thing that you went back to work, you stayed at home and looked after them unless you were a career woman, but now that is not true. Women are much more independent.

A lot of reason why women changed to Labour was they are working and more knowledgeable about politics than previously.

They are paying for the world and they want more of a say in it.

(Women voters, 1999)

Tony Blair, as the new leader of the Labour Party seemed to personify some of the positive changes. He was a youthful, 'family man', in touch through his own experience, with how women's lives had changed

He's got younger children and I think that relates more to people with families.

You feel that he understands how the likes of us live.

I think the fact that he has a wife who is still prepared to be an independent worker and a mother which is what most of us are now – you can relate to that, too.

They seem quite a normal couple.

(Women voters, 1999)

Blair is seen to avoid the 'talking shop' politics so disliked by women, and his general manner and approach is also much admired

When he talks you feel that he is getting straight to the point and not playing games – he just says what he wants to say without any point scoring and I really like that. (Woman voter 1999)

This contrasts sharply with Conservative leader, William Hague's approach, especially as seen in Prime Minister's Questions (in itself a short hand for what is wrong with the 'male' approach to politics: aggressive, self-serving adversarial performances rather than getting things done).

I hate all that sarcastic back chat – he's like a horrid little school boy! (Woman voter, 1999)

Finally, Labour's clear focus on the issues that really matter to women voters, especially on health and education, has been important in reinforcing that this is a new approach that is practical and hands on.

You felt that they were listening to what we wanted – a fresh start and action on the things that matter in our lives – schools and hospitals.

Labour are for more fundamental things like education, health, what your taxes are being paid for; providing for your children

(Women voters 1999)

How do women see the government now?

Women remain the most volatile proportion of the floating electorate. Immediately after the General Election in 1997, the enthusiasm of women who had switched allegiance reflected their belief that things were changing. Women in focus groups who, two weeks before, had not even been certain that they were going to vote, had become so euphoric that they had caught a mini cab into central London from the suburbs, to feel 'part' of the moment.

> We just did it – we said let's go down the Festival Hall and it was a fantastic atmosphere there – like a pop concert or something. Hundreds of people all cheering and waving. It felt like a fresh start for the whole country! (Woman voter, 1997)

Two and a half years on, Blair and his government remain popular, although women floating voters persist in being a tougher target than their male counterparts. Recent polling evidence shows that, in June 2000, the gender gap had not changed since May 1997. However, work conducted in November 99 by MORI for the *Times* was the first to show that women were significantly less likely than men to be 'satisfied' with the way that the Labour Government was running the country (-7 per cent). This point of view was more marked among women drawn from the key voter target age group, 35-44, (-13 per cent). Subsequent quantitative polling has continued to reflect this, suggesting a 'disatisfaction gap' consolidating at around 13 per cent.

The vulnerability of women's loyalty to Labour is clear from qualitative research, where the more anecdotal responses reveal a concern that the hoped for 'seismic shift' in political practice has not really happened. While men, more contented with the status quo, are happier to give the Government the benefit of the doubt and 'wait and see', women are impatient for change in two fundamental areas. Firstly, they are indignant at signs that the Government, despite its promise to 'do politics differently', has 'reverted to form': it's too much business as usual.

> I thought that they were going to be so different, but now I worry that they are just like all the others – out for themselves without any interest in the likes of us.

> Nothing's gone terribly wrong, but I suppose I just feel a bit let down – everything seemed so fresh and new, but now they just seem the same as the others.

> (Women voters 1999)

They are also impatient for positive change in the specific services where pledges have been made. Because they are on the practical, receiving end of that change, no amount of rhetoric will convince them that it has taken place if their own experience in the playground or hospital tells them otherwise. Men, who on the whole have less of this personal experience, make easier converts.

> In my kid's school there are still classes with up to 35 or 40 kids. They're nowhere near solving the problem.

> My mother's operation has been cancelled twice due to bed shortages – I think it's disgusting.

> (Women voters 1999)

Have more women MPs made a difference?

Much of the feminisation of the Labour Party has been rightly attributed personally to Tony Blair, and his strong, yet un-macho style of leadership. However, women voters are also very much aware of another symbolic feature of this Government: the increased number of women MPs, which is felt to have been very influential in shaping the key, positive differences in this government's approach. Women, with their more hands-on approach to the family and home, are thought to be better equipped than men to be politicians (in the new, more popular model that is both 'can do' and caring).

> Tony Blair has brought in a lot of women politicians, which has made a real difference

> Like I said, women and men are just made differently and they're (women) more likely to think about other people than men.

> They'll get on with it – get things done.

> More down to earth.

> Common sense.

> (Women voters, 1999)

Many of the more popular and well known figures within the Government are women (disproportionate in fact to their actual presence). Their influence, rightly or wrongly, is felt to be far reaching and symbolic of the way that Labour is changing politics

> Mo Mowlam is a good example of the good things about this government – she's very up front. She just gets on with it – doesn't care about herself, she's really genuine and gets things done. I think she's completely fantastic!

> Harriet Harman is fighting for working mums and she always has – I remember her breastfeeding her baby in the House of Commons. Because she's a Mum and she knows what it's like she's looking out for other Mums.

> (Women voters, 1999)

This is pointed up as a key difference between the Labour approach and the Conservative approach.

> The Tories seem to be more that it's a job for the boys – a closed shop.

> William Hague wouldn't dare to bring a load of women in like Tony Blair has – he couldn't hack it.

> He's too busy thinking of clever clever things to say in parliament.

> (Women voters, 1999)

This view reflects a further change in women's views. In the past women believed that the gender of their political representative was irrelevant. This may still be true when assessing the ability of an individual politician; however, when politicians are seen *en masse*, how representative they are now matters very much.

This change can be attributed to a number of reasons – most importantly, it reflects the changes in women voters' own lives. In the days when fewer women worked outside the home, women politicians were so different from them that they reflected their own life experiences, if anything, even less accurately than men.

> They (women politicians) earn a fortune and have nannies and everything – they don't have a clue how people like us live. (Woman voter 1986)

However, given the way that women's lives have changed, this cultural gap no longer exists and a working mum is a working mum whether she is a politician or hairdresser.

They understand juggling – they may have more money but the problems don't go away. (Woman voter 1999)

The unfinished revolution

So women see the increased number of Labour women politicians as an important step – one that symbolises how the party has changed. However, it is vital to realise that this is a *first* step,: a statement of intent that will start to move the Party to what is now regarded as an obvious objective: equal representation.

It's got to be 50/50 – why should it be anything else?

It would be really good if it was half and half – I think that's what they said they would do.

I think that they've had to realise that now because women are coming into their own, having to work and run houses and it's a changing world – it's not dominated by men any more.

(Women voters 1999)

In this context, women recognise the difficulties faced by women trying to enter politics, and are more prepared than ever before to support the development of strategies to help them, ranging from different education to positive discrimination and quotas.

It is so much harder for women, like it is at work.

It's still like a working man's club.

It needs to start in school – girls need to be told they can do it – they don't have to be a secretary.

They need a crèche in the Houses of Parliament.

They should just say half our MPs are going to be women! What's wrong with that?

I think that women lack a lot of confidence... I would love to go into politics but I know it would be such an uphill struggle and so many closed doors...those doors have to be opened for more women.

(Women voters 1999)

The corollary of this is that if Labour does not continue on this supposed route or, worse still, is perceived to move in the wrong direction, this would be interpreted as a negative, backwards step.

If they go back to all men, it would be like back to the cloth cap image again wouldn't it!

It will also be important that women are not only a force in terms of numbers, but that they are visible – seen to be playing an important role.

I read that Mo Mowlam is thinking of leaving politics. In some ways you can't blame her after all she's been through, but we need women like her – she's in touch with us.

I think they'd go back to their old ways.

They'd never get things done for health and education, because I don't really think they (men) care about those things.

(Women voters 1999)

There has been a revolution in the life of Worcester Woman, taking her out of the home and transforming her expectations of the world around her. The Labour Party has also undergone a revolution that has apparently reflected this experience and, in doing so, has won her confidence and her vote. But polling data consistently demonstrates that women remain more sceptical of Labour than men. The qualitative research evidence shows that they are anxious that the radical changes that have taken place, enabling them to vote Labour, are not lasting. A 'quick fix' will be no substitute for a sustainable new approach to politics – one that is practical, 'can do' and focused on the things that matter. This is Worcester Woman's unfinished revolution.

6. Representing difference: why should it matter if women get elected?

Anne Phillips

By the beginning of the 20th century, women's right to vote had become one of the major political issues, dividing party from party and women from women as well as women from men. By the beginning of the 21st century, women's right to vote on equal terms with men has been extended into a wider claim about representation. We do not just demand the equal right to vote and stand for election (a right that might still deliver legislatures composed exclusively of men). Many of us have come to believe that fair representation means equal representation, and that elected bodies should be drawn roughly equally from both women and men.

The shift, in fact, took less than a century, for while the equal right to vote was only recognised by one country (New Zealand) in 1900, and hasn't been recognised by Saudi Arabia to this day, the idea that fair representation means a rough parity of elected positions between women and men has been gaining ground for a good thirty years. Political parties in the Nordic countries took the lead in this, setting in place a variety of mechanisms to ensure more women stood for election; and citizens living in Sweden or Norway or Denmark have now become accustomed to cabinets where women hold half the positions and parliaments where they make up 35-40 per cent. The UK leapt up the league table in 1997 with an intake of 120 women MPs, an achievement that doubled the previous proportion of women in parliament to an unprecedented 18.4 per cent. But the UK is still put into the shade by Sweden (42.7 per cent), Germany (30.9 per cent), South Africa (30 per cent), Australia (22.4 per cent); and only ranks 25 in the world table compiled by the Inter-Parliamentary Union (IPU, 2000). The point to note about such figures is that none of the more dramatic ones can be put down to accident. Most countries have managed a gradual increase in the number of women in parliament, reflecting a declining prejudice against women or an increase in the number of women in professional jobs. All the speedier transformations, however, have come about through political action and as a result of feminist campaigns.

The extent and the extraordinary success, compared with some other feminist causes, of these campaigns suggests we are living through a period when women's empowerment and women's equality are very much to the forefront of the political agenda. The puzzle is that the initiatives coincide (in Britain but also elsewhere) with a marked complacency about women's position. This comes out in comments about a 'post-feminist' age where gender politics has allegedly become redundant; or in agitated anxiety about the crisis of masculinity and declining position of men. Some of this reflects the strange perception that women achieve equality with men when they become somewhat less subordinate: a peculiar misreading of the notion of equality that should alert us to the continuing power of assumptions about it being 'normal' for women to be lesser than men. We might add to this that strategies devoted to changing those at the top (more women in parliament, more women in management, more women with professional careers) are always potentially misleading because they focus attention on what is most visible, leaving less glamorous inequalities in the shade. The point I want to develop here is that the coexistence of ambitious initiatives on women's political representation with complacency about women's position also testifies to deep ambiguity about why we need more women in parliament (Phillips, 1995). If this ambiguity is not recognised and addressed, the moves towards fairer representation will be less far-reaching than many of us have hoped.

The right to equal opportunity

Why does the under-representation of women matter? Why should it matter whether our representatives are women or men? One answer to this fits within a broad framework of equal opportunities: the idea that women should have the same chances as men to serve as political representatives and to pursue their political careers. By what possible superiority of either talent or experience could men claim the 'right' to monopolise decision-making assemblies? There is, so far as we know, no genetic reason why women should be less suited to the tasks of political representation, less capable of arguing a case, representing the views of their constituents, and contributing to the decision-making process. That being so, we should expect a roughly random distribution between the sexes when candidates are being chosen to contest elections or elected to carry out the representative's role. That the actual distribution is far from random confirms what all of us already know: that it is far harder for women than men to off-load their caring responsibilities, harder for women than men to present themselves as figures of authority, harder for women than men to take their own political aspirations seriously. The background inequalities are obvious enough, but instead of treating these as excuses or explanations, we should regard them as making a mockery of women's supposedly equal right. Failing additional measures (like the all-women short-lists employed by the Labour Party before the last general election, or the numerical quotas employed by a large number of political parties across the contemporary world), women do not have the same opportunities as men.

This is a commendable and radical argument (and more radical than current Labour Party policy, which has abandoned all-women short lists without offering anything in their place). It makes us more acutely aware that the current distribution of influence and power is indefensible; it gives no credence to self-serving claims about this distribution being normal and natural; and it encourages us to do something about it. There are plenty of people who will shake their heads in sorrow at the unhappy state of affairs that leaves us with so few women in parliament, but nonetheless back away from any decisive action. They regard the statistics as unfortunate but understandable, something they just hope will eventually change. In contrast to this, most of the arguments for women's representation have developed a strong version of equal opportunities that takes issue with more standard oppositions between equality of opportunity and equality of outcome. If the outcome is assemblies dominated by men, then the opportunities were clearly not equal; legal equality alone does not establish equality of choice.

The argument for 'real' equality of opportunity is sometimes combined with more general points about the symbolic impact of legislatures that are dominated by men, the way these depict men as the active participants while infantilising women as the objects of their care. Both arguments figure large in popular views about the unfairness of male dominance in politics – but neither of them says much about what women representatives are expected to do. Indeed in many ways, they merely extend to political office the argument we might also apply to women in management or the professions: the notion that women should have the same chance as men to pursue interesting and rewarding careers. Those campaigning for more women in politics have often made their case in a particularly radical way (insisting on affirmative action, for example, to guarantee the equality, rather than leaving the equality up to chance), but so long as the argument is phrased in terms of equal opportunities, it does not engage with what is special about representation. If we think, as most of us probably do, that being a political representative is not just a job like any other, and that politicians should not be in public life just to further their own careers, then equating the right to be an MP with the right to be a boxer or barrister rings rather hollow. Of course women should have the same chances as men – but isn't there more to the argument than that?

Representing different experiences

The extra is where the difficulties begin, for the more profound reason for promoting the better representation of women – as also for promoting the better representation of citizens from ethnic and racial minorities – is that different groups have different experiences, perspectives, needs and interests, and that those who remain outside the political process are unlikely to get their needs or interests addressed. It used to be thought (but only because we didn't think long about it) that anyone could represent anyone else. In the context of sustained inequalities between male and female, white and black, this is an absurdly optimistic idea. When people recoil from images of an all-white parliament determining the laws and policies for a population made up of both white and black, this is not just because such a scenario could only develop in a grotesquely unfair society. (It is not, that is, just because such an outcome proves to us that the opportunities were far from equal.) The unease also testifies to a well-founded suspicion about the decisions this sort of parliament will take. The intuition underpinning virtually all initiatives to change the composition of legislative bodies is that people are fallible, limited, and partial, that our political priorities and judgements are framed by our life-histories and location, and that with the best will in the world, we tend to see things from our own point of view. Many democracies protect their citizens against the self-seeking bias of elected politicians by drawing up a Bill of Rights, to be interpreted by the wisest of judges; but judges can also be partial, and their experience of life is often rather weird. The best safeguard against partiality and bias is the inclusion of all relevant groups in the decision-making assembly, and the opportunity this gives for all those likely to be affected to contribute their ideas and concerns. It is for this reason, more than any other, that that we so urgently need women representatives as well as men, representatives from the ethnic minority as well as ethnic majority. We need them because we cannot trust the judgements of an assembly from which they are absent. We need them to bring their different experiences to bear.

Some experiences are, of course, more detachable than others, and there are cases where it seems plausible enough to talk of representation by individuals who were not directly exposed. I find it relatively easy to think of a well-informed agricultural expert as representing the interests of farmers (though I can see I might think differently if I were a farmer), but I find it less plausible to think of a well-informed male expert on gender as representing the perspectives of women. This is partly because perspectives attach, by their very definition, to those looking from a particular location, and partly because of the power relations involved. Where there has been a long history of subordination, exclusion or denial, it seems particularly inappropriate to look to individuals without such experience as spokespeople for the group: not because individuals outside the group can never be knowledgeable or never be trusted, but because without the direct involvement of those with the relevant experiences, the policy process will be inherently paternalistic and the outcomes almost certainly skewed. Embodiment matters. By their presence in a decision-making assembly, members of a previously marginalised group can better guarantee that their interests and perspectives will be articulated. By their presence, they also make it more likely that members of previously dominant groups will recognise and speak to their concerns.

It will be apparent to anyone that these arguments are at odds with current understandings of representation– and certainly at odds with the way the Labour Party perceives its role. In the conventions of party politics, candidates may be, and often are, selected partly on the basis of personal attributes. Thus, one candidate may be favoured over another because of a particularly close connection with the locality;

because he shares certain key characteristics with the local population; or because she comes from an under-represented group – like women – whose profile the party is keen to raise. In some cases, possession of these attributes will be used to advantage in the election campaign, and voters will be encouraged to regard the candidate more favourably because of them. At the moment of election, however, it is assumed that we vote not for individuals but for parties (a correct enough assumption in the British case), and those elected are then charged not with representing their group but with promoting their party's policies and concerns. Having played with the idea that difference matters, most parties (and many politicians) then recoil from the idea that individuals might be elected so as to represent that difference, and at this point we hear all the usual disclaimers about representing everyone, or promoting the so-called 'common good'.

A puzzling double imperative

This generates a puzzling double imperative – one may be selected so as to reflect the different experiences and perspectives of a previously under-represented group, but one is elected to represent a political party – and it is in the context of this puzzle that we can best understand the difficulties experienced by some of the newly elected women MPs in the 1997 Parliament. A significant number of the new Labour MPs were selected by constituencies that were keen to address women's under-representation in politics. They were selected, then, at least partly on the basis of their gender. All of them, however, were elected as candidates of the Labour Party, with no obvious mandate to speak for anything else. How, then, could they legitimately challenge the Government's decision to end special benefits for single parents – the first major issue on which all those extra women in parliament might have been expected to make some difference? By what right could they set up their own views against those of the Party? Were they there to represent women or represent Labour?

Commenting on the much longer history of women's representation in Norway, and the very similar tensions that have emerged there between representing what they may perceive as in the interests of women and supporting their party's line, Hege Skjeie warns against what she calls the rhetoric of difference: 'The belief in women's difference could still turn into a mere litany on the importance of difference. Repeated often enough, the statement that "gender matters" may in turn convince the participants that change can in fact be achieved by no other contribution than the mere presence of women' (Skjeie, 1991). Yet if simply being there is all that it is about, we have nothing more than a rather glorified argument about equal opportunities: the belief that it is fairer to have some women alongside the men.

There is a tension, in other words, between the representation of difference – the representation of those multiple differences of experience associated with positions in a gender, racial or class hierarchy – and the representation by political party. If political parties fail to address this tension, they will end up with the mere window-dressing of brighter clothes and softer voices. When you ask people why they want more women in parliament, they will usually say they think women representatives will behave differently from men, that women will bring a different range of experiences to bear on decisions, will prioritise different policy areas, perhaps even be less dogmatic and aggressive, more prepared to listen to other points of view. They expect, in other words, that women will do more or other than men. If the constraints of party representation block this – if each representative is expected to vote and act exactly like any other representative from the same party – then the difference supposedly attached to gender fades into insignificance. More women becomes simply more women. This may be a good development in terms of equal opportunities. It does not, in any grander sense, further women's political inclusion.

Evidence suggests that there are indeed significant differences between women and men when it comes to policy priorities, and that there are particularly significant differences when it comes to issues of equality between women and men (Norris, 1996). Having more women in Parliament then opens up space for a different range of concerns to enter into the process of policy formation, and having more women in the Cabinet raises hopes that these concerns will be more seriously addressed. But measures to promote women's political representation can only deliver on this wider promise if parties accept that it is legitimate for women representatives to act in this way. This means welcoming rather than silencing what may be seen as voices of internal dissent, and backing off from tight party discipline. I do not mean by this that women politicians should be freed up to pursue only their own personal agendas, or that if they do so they will automatically represent something called 'the interests of women'. Taken to extremes, the first would undermine the principles of accountability that are crucial to any democracy, making a mockery of the election process and turning party programmes into a grim joke. The second is patently at odds with everything we know about the diversity of women, a diversity not just of experiences but also of political views. But if there is a problem about the under-representation of women, and the problem is bigger than not enough women getting a fair crack at a political career, it cannot be solved through numbers alone. It has to be possible for women MPs to articulate what may be conflicts of interest. It has to be possible for them to do something different from what would otherwise have been done.

Transforming democracy

In my own rather cynical reading, New Labour has embraced some of the arguments about women's representation because it sees a feminised party as more attractive to women voters. It also finds the feminisation of the party particularly helpful in marking the distance from the masculine traditions of 'old' Labour. But New Labour has been less enthusiastic about the deeper critique of our system of democracy that points to the exclusion of women's experiences, needs or perspectives – a critique that sees the fairer representation of women as a way of transforming policy concerns. Recognising the second means recognising the bias and exclusions that pervade current policy formation. It means taking more seriously what Iris Marion Young discusses as the hegemonic power of dominant groups (Young, 1990). It means acknowledging the key role of the previously excluded in articulating new policies and concerns.

What we have at present is an uncomfortable half-way house, where more women in politics is seen as a good thing but a good thing that somehow stops there. We can make a powerful enough case for more women in politics without attaching to this any expectation of further change (women have an equal right to participate in politics even if what they do with it turns out to be indistinguishable from the men), but the hope that has underpinned decades of feminist campaigning is that women can represent experiences and interests that have for too long been ignored. This implies a level of self-criticism and humility that comes hard to most political parties – it is always easier to believe 'we' already know what policies are best – and an openness to alternatives that presumes much of the work is still to be done. Tackling women's under-representation should be seen as the beginning rather than the end of the process, not something we celebrate as 'proof' that the two sexes are now equal, but something that enables that crucial next stage.

At this moment in British history, we cannot even be confident that the first task will be completed, for while policies of 'twinning' constituencies so as to ensure greater parity of representation have brought gender equality far closer in the Scottish Parliament and Welsh Assembly, there is little evidence of similar policies being considered for elections to the House of Commons. Tempting as it may then be to fall back on more straightforward arguments about equality of opportunity, this would be a misplaced strategy. If gender matters, it is because men and women still occupy very different positions within social and economic relations; and what matters about this is that it generates different interests and different policy concerns. Numbers alone are important, but the longer term significance lies in the opportunity for mobilising a wider range of voices, articulating concerns that would otherwise be discounted, and thereby developing more just social policies. It will be hard to do this unless political parties admit that they do not have all the answers already.

References

Inter-Parliamentary Union (2000) website on Women in National Parliaments www.ipu.org/wmn-e/classif.htm

Norris P (1996) 'Women Politicians: Transforming Westminster?' in Lovenduski J and Norris P (eds) *Women in Politics* Oxford: Oxford University Press.

Phillips A (1995) *The Politics of Presence:The Political Representation of Gender, Ethnicity and Race* Oxford: Oxford University Press.

Skjeie H (1991) 'The Rhetoric of Difference: On Women's Inclusion Into Political Elites' in *Politics and Society* 19/2: 258

Young I M (1990) *Justice and the Politics of Difference* Princeton: Princeton University Press.

7. Ain't I a woman? The need for a new dialogue about gender and diversity

Yasmin Alibhai-Brown

> My own search over the years has certainly been based on an effort to reveal suppressed possibilities – those understandings that time rushes past but which can also be a means of releasing aspiration. (Rowbotham, 1997)

For many years now I have travelled uneasily between the politics of identity and feminism, loosely defined and in all its forms. I am in both locations of struggle which unfortunately still only relate to each other negatively or with suspicion. Questions constantly arise and there is nobody to answer them satisfactorily. Why are all leading feminists white and what does that say about their theories, methods and approach? Why have black women allowed themselves to be relegated to the margins? Why do they not see their own lives in mainstream terms? And finally and most importantly, what are the key areas where an understanding of race, ethnicity and gender are crucial in any credible analysis of what has happened, or may hapen in the future.

Women in Britain – white, black and Asian – have been at the front line of the mammoth social changes in Britain that escalated after the second world war. These were happening at the same time as further tremors of the women's movement in the West began to be felt. Women learnt that getting the vote was only the beginning and not the end of the struggle for equality. Just like the end of Empire was never going to be the end of that struggle for black and Asian Britons. We have never understood these fundamental connections. I am an East African Asian, a twice removed involuntary migrant with at least three cultural cross currents within me. My mother had to do three jobs to keep us fed while my father dreamed his dreams. She had feminism thrust upon her long before the word was invented. At one time I had to cope with the intolerable burden of being a lone mother abandoned by her partner in a community where such things were rare and always the fault of the woman who could not keep her man happy. I have a son who is big, brown and bold and who will therefore always be seen as a threat and an object of hatred, leaving me, like many black and Asian mothers living in constant terror. The cases of Stephen Lawrence, Ricky Reel and countless others have only intensified these anxieties. Rearing children in this atmosphere is so tough I sometimes wonder how we have had the courage to reproduce at all. Added to all the moods and furies of teenage life, your child hates you for bringing him or her into this country or regards you as inferior or worst of all turns to self destructive acts because he/she expected to be embraced by this society and was rejected instead and there is no place to go. What is more, it is a thankless task that our men have mostly left to us. Most modern feminists have no idea of the impact of such burdens.

Yet long before large scale immigration from the New Commonwealth, many white women had established bonds with black people on these shores. White prostitutes and ordinary women in London and the slave ports harboured and took up with escaped slaves in the 16th and 17th centuries. Through the years that followed, many white women carried on this tradition of crossing the menacing and strictly demarcated racial boundaries on this island. Their men were none too pleased. Sexism mingled with racism to create a potent, explosive mix which, between 1911 and 1958, erupted in skirmishes and even riots on the streets. The American writer Beth Day described such attitudes (which were even more dramatically on display in the US) in a passionate, polemical book. She wrote:

> One of the sad features…is that the white women never did ask to be protected from those black men. It was their fathers', husbands' and brothers' idea. White women were as much victims of the system as black men. (Day, 1974)

In the acclaimed Channel Four series, White Tribe, the presenter Darcus Howe, acknowledged that white women, then and now, have been crucial in the development of multicultural Britain (Howe, 2000).

In fact, women in all the communities of Britain have always been significantly over-represented among those who challenge social codes, historical and political relationships, and martyr themselves if necessary to make their case. The rules which define their lives were never of their making and most to this day still have little power to overhaul systems and beliefs which have been set down by male prophets, politicians, fathers, husbands and brothers.

This means that racism and sexism, feminism and anti-racism (not to mention class), have been tangled up for as long as the historical eye can read, only most of us seem only to be able to keep our eyes on one of the threads. These are not additional burdens along the same continuum of disadvantage – the so-called theories of double and triple jeopardy. The woven threads embody complex configurations, subtle identity and identification changes which take place in the course of a single conversation so that Black and white women can have intensely similar reactions to one situation and vastly different ones to another. Demographic developments make it absurd to talk along colour lines. What, for example, about the growing number of white women, like Sandra, with mixed race children?:

> I started women's studies as an access student. I learnt about power and men and women. My man was African and very macho and I knew that often the reason he was abusive was because he found it so hard to get the respect he deserved. But he was beating me and the kids up. I couldn't ever

discuss this even in my own mind because it seemed so racist. Then he just disappeared after giving me a right pasting which left my eye damaged. I felt so confused and would have liked to talk to black women about this.' [1]

Six out of ten 'Caribbean' children have one white parent which means either a white mother or a white father, each bringing a batch of such issues to confront. There are stepfamilies where white men are learning to parent black children. Feminism has influenced young Asian women who are choosing to marry white men instead of Asian men in order – they think – to have more autonomous lives. Many black women are deeply disappointed by black men and are also marrying out.

Missing conversations

With so much to share, why is this essential discourse between Black, Asian and white women not taking place? This may be partly because many white women are uninterested or too ready to exploit the information for their own ends (as journalists, for example), or to rush to enlighten or rescue us from our communities. But there are also some benign reasons for this distancing. Perhaps some white women – especially those who feel deeply about racism, exclusion and justice – are scared of treading in places they are not wanted or they don't know how to behave. (This anxiety exists mainly among white urban professional white women. During the course of doing interviews for my book *Who Do We Think We Are?* I found natural and open friendships between white and black women locked into a life on benefits, under-education and little hope of escape.) Could it be that the reasons for this split between politicized black and white women is less to do with arrogance or myopia and more to do with the fact that many white feminists feel there are real and often insurmountable barriers between us?

On the other side, many educated black women do not wish to make the links between their lives and those of white women because of racism. Others go even further than this. You go along to some meetings and you still hear that all the male oppression that black and Asian women suffer from is the work of the white imperialist devil. Still others deny any common humanity between white women and themselves and cling on to the idea of identity as if it were pure, historically fixed, homogeneous.

This is not to underplay the genuine dilemmas and obvious tensions between cultural autonomy and gender equality; between racism and sexism; between the priorities of powerful white women and powerless white and Black women; between the achievements of the women's movement in three decades and the new problems brought about by those achievements. For decades now, our concerns as Black women have just been swept into nothingness, like sighs in a storm as we gather for comfort among our own in our own back rooms. Post feminists who claim grand political power, because they wear strappy sandals and hot red lipstick, sound intolerably presumptuous to many black and Asian women.

In fact, most writers on this issue in Britain in recent years have failed to include the lives and thoughts of black and Asian women. Look at this very incomplete list taken within a single year. When that brilliant Observer writer (and a friend, still, I hope) Nicci Gerard wrote a scathing essay on the sisterhood, she forgot to mention that she was really only describing the white female experience, both here and in the United States. Ditto Decca Aitkinhead, Maureen Freely, Charlotte Raven.[2] What about including the perspectives of radical filmmaker Pratibha Parmar, or the writings of Parminder Bacchu, Amina Mama or Kum Kum Bhavnani, Heidi Mirza?

There are exceptions. Traditional feminists such as Germaine Greer and Gloria Steinham have, throughout their lives, made links with different forms of oppression. Women's editors and journalists on the liberal papers have been also been open to our influence. They include Suzanne Moore, Sally Weale, Hilly Janes, Claire Longrigg, Melissa Benn, Yvonne Roberts, Katherine Viner, Libby Brookes who do manage to incorporate and include us without patronizing, by trying to understand the deepest impulses of our lives. In academia, especially in Women's Studies there is a unselfconscious incorporation of culture and race within gender considerations, as at the University of Hull, where programmes run by Kathleen Lennon do this as a matter of course. More recent work by such authors as Morwena Griffiths are also distinguished by the commitment with which they make connections.

> In the past feminists have had a dream of sisterhood and a common language. Recognition of hybridity and multilingualism shows that, so far from this being desirable, differences between women and their different languages combined with the points of overlap between them, actually improve the possibilities of political change. (Griffiths, 1995)

But this is still rare. There are dozens of other feminists who assume a colourless position and believe that to be unproblematic, making no attempts to expand the world they are describing (Figes, 1994; Hewitt, 1993).

Divided we fall

We – Black British women – would carry on regardless if the only problems we faced were at the level of theory, ideology and cultural understanding. What is unacceptable is that these attitudes affect our daily lives, our rights and struggles to survive and grow. White women, especially middle class white women now occupy more powerful positions in British society than ever before. They still have their battles of course to reach the parts that men get to often without effort. Or talent. But many of these women who have climbed to near the top do not seem to display much need or desire to carry us with them.

The involvement of white women is required in crucial areas. If they only knew and accepted this responsibility. Immigration and asylum laws have a particularly harrowing effect on women and even positive changes can impact negatively on women – something that may be unknown to policy makers, because Black women are usually not consulted. For instance; the Labour government, rightly, abolished the primary purpose rule which discriminated against black and Asian women wanting to marry someone from abroad. What the government would not have known without consulting Black women is that many Asian girls used the rule to avoid forced marriages. Black women are among the most active and highly educated people in the labour force and yet they are denied access to top jobs even in areas where they form a central part of the workforce like in the nursing profession. And though some Indian, African and Afro-Caribbean women are doing well in the labour market, most of the rest are still having to fight each step of the way for their basic rights (Unison, 1997). Should not such fights be at the heart of feminism? And if they are not, why should black and Asian women give a toss about how many white women are on the board of News International or Marks and Spencers?

In politics our neglect is reflected strikingly in New Labour politics. As a woman I was elated (and still am) to see the influx of women into parliament in the 1997 election. But dragging down that elation were the questions about why in this year of all years, we black and Asian women hardly increased our presence. Oona King, is half African American and half Jewish. Dianne Abbot is one of our most intelligent MPs. She has the same straight speaking qualities of Clare Short. How many white feminists have ever spoken up for Abbott the way some of them have when Short or Harman have been treated with contempt by the party or by the media?

There is another difficult area to be explored. What are we to make of the real (sometimes surely deliberate) discrimination that we are now seeing perpetrated by white women against black and Asian women? As the keynote speaker at three conferences (UNISON Black women in the Workplace, NUT Black Teachers Conference, and London Voluntary Organisations Network) I repeatedly heard tales of cruelty and racism directed at Black nurses, teachers, local authority workers (including within Equalities teams) and voluntary sector workers. The perpetrators were all white women.

Having more white women in power has not been a panacea for us or indeed for most other white women. But are we, Black women, being narrow minded? Is our own inclusion not implicit and is that not better than forced entry by tokenism? In some ways this is like asking Cinders to have generosity enough to take pleasure in her sisters' good fortune and it does not address the thoughtless, automatic neglect of women of colour in any grand narrative on feminism or womanhood. On the other hand, many black women have no empathy with white women trapped in poverty, or violent relationships or, more generally, a cruel life of powerlessness. To be white is not to be right but neither should it mean that you are by definition all right. Black and Asian women who have thrown themselves on the pyres of 'culture' have defended the indefensible in the name of diversity. Fourteen year old British Asian girls are locked up, beaten, exported to Pakistan, India or Bangladesh forced into marriages. Hundreds of black women are abandoned by the fathers of their children and dare not speak too loud because that is thought to be treacherous.

The need for a new dialogue

I would like to see in our public spaces the kinds of important debate that are taking place in the United States and elsewhere about cultural group rights and gender equality. Women like Susan Moller Okin and Leila Ahmed speak out with a freedom on these thorny issues in ways that would be unthinkable in the UK (Moller Okin, 1997; Ahmed, 1992). Likewise, Black feminists like Alice Walker are not sectarian in the way they think, nor are Indian feminists like Madhu Kishwar and Shabana Azmi.

I would also like us be able to converse about common concerns. I fear my daughter will pick up the sexual freedoms of the West which have done us no good at all. Instead of saying no all the time, women and girls are now encouraged – from the age of ten – to proffer up pierced bellies, wonderbra boobs, slits and slashes, perfect bodies for boys and men who seem increasingly addicted to the idea of sex everywhere and any time, on tap. Such conversations are not about cultural divides although they are often presented that way.

How can we Black women connect with mainstream issues and powerful white people – especially feminists – without being appropriated, embittered or silenced? And how we can remain true to our difference while judging our own communities through some universal humanistic standards. We need to get white feminists to be as self critical and open as some of us are now prepared to be about ourselves. Razia Aziz, an impressive new feminist, says that she will not play today's game by yesterday's rules, whereby:

> the energetic assertion of black/white (or any other) difference tends to create fixed and oppositional categories which can result in another version of the suppression of difference. Differences *within* categories – here black and white – are underplayed in order to establish it between them. Consequently, each category takes on a deceptive air of internal coherence and similarities between women in different groups are thus suppressed.
> (Crowley and Himmelweit, 1992)

To conclude, Black and white women, whether feminists or not, must develop a new relationship beyond individual friendships. White feminists need to listen more and show greater humility and courage and also to check out their own non-negotiable principles because women of colour are increasingly as likely to question them as are many men of all hues. White feminists have infinitely more power and influence than do Black women and they must take responsibility for changing the way the world has treated Black women. Black feminists and Black women in general also have decisions to make. Are they a part of womanhood or are they apart from it in some exotic imagined place of their own? Have they played a part in their own marginalisation and do they now have to break free from a culture of separation to a more equal, participatory and difficult relationship with their white sisterhood? We have so much to talk about. And feminism must surely lie at the heart of these conversations, even if most women these days wouldn't be seen dead wearing the label. As Heidi Mirza has commented, the black feminist critique engendered a guilty paralysis among white feminists for over twenty years:

> This needs to be intercepted if feminism is to move forward. Feminism as a term, as movement is not impervious to change. If feminism changes to embrace differences rather than be preoccupied with difference, then its meaning will change and strengthen black and white feminist activism through a unified and cohesive and strategic identity (Mirza 1998).

Endnotes

1   Interview with the author.

2   This refers to articles by these authors that appeared, respectively in the *Observer* (2.4.97) and the *Guardian* (13.5.97, 5.1.98 and 9.9.96).

References

Ahmed L (1992) *Women and Gender in Islam* Yale University Press

Crowley H and Himmelweit S (eds) (1992) *Knowing Women: Feminism and Knowledge* London: Polity Press, p293

Day B (1974) *Sexual life between blacks and whites* London: Collins, p8

Figes K (1994) *Of Her Sex* London: Macmillan,

Griffiths M (1995) *Feminism and the Self* London: Routledge, p182

Hewitt P (1993) *About time: The Revolution in Work and Family Life* London: Institute for Public Policy Research

Howe D (2000) Channel Four Television, 25 January.

Mirza H (1998) *Black British Feminism* Routledge, p18.

Moller Okin S (1997) 'Is Multiculturalism Bad For Women' in *The Boston Review* October.

Rowbotham S (1997) *A Century of Women* London: Viking, p580

Unison (1997) *Black Women's Employment and Pay* London: Unison, March

8. A new start in Wales: how devolution is making a difference
Val Feld

The notion of a 'third way' sitting somewhere between traditional socialism and capitalism is not a concept that resonates easily in Welsh politics. Although there are probably a hundred different definitions, the badge of 'socialism' is worn with pride by the majority of Labour members and supporters, and is also claimed by some Liberal Democrats and Plaid Cymru activists. Whilst most of us still espouse the aims and values of traditional democratic socialism, the modernisers of Welsh politics would reject the centralised paternalism, narrow dogma and inability to value diversity that used to characterise Labour in Wales.

Equality of opportunity has long been a core value for those on the left. But while the rhetoric is easy, there have been few signs in existing political institutions of any willingness on the part of men to give up power and enable women to achieve the more significant objective of equality of outcome. Nor has there been the kind of radical change in the culture or practice of existing institutions that would lead to the agenda and working practices for which Labour women have argued. In the campaigning and debate that preceded the establishment of the National Assembly for Wales there was always the proviso, particularly among Labour pro-devolutionists, that it must usher in a new politics. Central to this new politics was to be substantial representation and influence from women.

The history of the Labour movement in Wales, enormous and far reaching though its influence has been, offers few heroines or female leaders although women were always the loyal and reliable troops in every political campaign. As many of the more difficult and testing struggles, such as the 1984-5 Miners Strike and the camps at Greenham Common showed, it was the women of Wales who often demonstrated the nerve, imagination and staying power. And yet, until May 1997 there had only ever been four women members of Parliament from Wales. Women-only shortlists, generally seen as distasteful, were imposed in seats where Labour had limited hope of success. In fact, the landslide victory raised the numbers of Welsh women MPs from one out of 40 to four – all Labour.

The local council elections in May 1999, despite publicity to attract more women and stringent interview procedures in the Labour Party, barely changed the percentage of around 20 per cent female councillors. Out of 22 councils, two women (one Plaid Cymru and one Independent) were elected leaders. Local government in Wales remains overwhelmingly elderly, white and male.

Breaking through to equal representation

It is in the National Assembly that the great breakthrough and change has been accomplished. This was not an easy victory. Labour politics in Wales has been dominated by the trade unions, traditionally representing substantially male workforces, and by powerful Labour local authority leaders. Welsh Labour leaders could realistically aspire to long and unchallenged political careers in both Westminster houses. It is hard to characterise politics in Wales as either new or old Labour. Many would say it is 'traditional', or as Rhodri Morgan has described himself, 'classic' Labour. Steeped in the working class collective history of the Labour movement, Welsh Labour politics was generally paternal, fiercely partisan and tribal, built on strong values of community, public service and fairness. A Welsh saying which resonates deep into the psyche is *chwarae teg* – in English 'fair play'. Unlike England where it is associated with the cricket pitch and public school good sportsmanship, in Wales the words have a sense of fundamental social justice and equality. It is perhaps because of the central importance of these values to the Welsh Labour movement that any suggestion that women did not receive 'fair play' and experienced discrimination would often provoke genuine hurt and anger, certainly amongst older Labour members.

For Labour pro-devolutionists it was always important that devolution opened out the political process so that power was genuinely passed closer to people. Equally necessary was challenging the long established system of patronage through the Welsh Office and local government and to develop opportunities for genuine political debate. Taking a lead from Scotland in the 1980s, the Campaign for a Welsh Assembly aspired at an early stage to equal representation of women and men. The original Labour Party Wales plan for the Assembly envisaged 80 seats, two per constituency, with each returning one man and one woman. This was generally perceived as fair. When in 1996 Tony Blair and Ron Davies decided to cut the Assembly to 60 and introduce proportional representation, the aspiration remained (although the wording in Labour Party documents became ambiguous). As a means to embed the principle, Labour equality campaigners then linked this notion to a commitment that the Assembly should have a responsibility to drive forward equality issues. For the first time it was proposed that the sex and race anti-discrimination requirements, previously only a UK-level duty, would be located in the workings and objectives of the Assembly. This was ultimately achieved through sections 48 and 120 of the Government of Wales Act, placing upon the Assembly a duty to have regard to equal opportunities in the way it conducts its business and functions. This is reinforced by the duty in s.120 (2) of the Government of Wales Act to publish an annual report outlining the impact of its activities on equal opportunities. These requirements have been important in ensuring that operating practices, policy and programme development are informed by equality considerations.

The aspiration of equal representation of women and men in the Assembly was achieved uniquely by Labour. Unable to follow the original plan for 'fair play', the Welsh Labour Party, with considerable pressure and encouragement from the National Executive, engaged in a highly acrimonious and nail biting internal battle for a plan to 'twin' constituencies. The experience of this struggle served to politicise and awaken many Labour women to the lengths to which some men (and some women) were willing to go to resist change. In the end Labour was the only party to field equal numbers of male and female candidates and achieved a record 16 women in a group of 29 – one more than half. The resignation of Alun Michael from May 2000 adds another woman from the regional list, bringing the total to 17 women and 15 men.

By luck rather than design the Liberal Democrat group of six comprises three men and three women. Plaid Cymru having promised to deliver equal numbers, lost their nerve when it appeared that their senior men would lose out, and compromised by placing women at the top of their regional lists ending up with six women out of 17. Only the Tories, opposed as always to any positive action, and now deeply embarrassed, elected no women in their group of nine.

The Welsh Assembly is uniquely placed, with women comprising 40 per cent of its membership (higher than any political institution outside Sweden) and a statutory responsibility to have regard to equality matters in its business. Alun Michael's first Cabinet included equal numbers of women and men, Rhodri Morgan, as First Secretary has gone further and now has more women than men. This is unique, we believe, in the Western world!

Changing the culture and content of politics

So, what difference has all this made to the nature and style of the political process? There is clear evidence of a significant influence on the seriousness with which gender (and indeed other) equality issues are treated. Family friendly hours for meetings – 9.00 to 5.30 – are strictly adhered too. In an institution with a substantial proportion of the members away from home during the days of sitting, there is a legitimate debate about what constitutes family friendly working hours. But the important difference is that it is taken as read that this is a serious issue. So, too, is childcare. Members have access to a crèche and the new National Assembly building will incorporate childcare facilities. Both the male and female toilets on the ground floor have nappy changing facilities – although as one (Tory) AM pointed out, both signs show a woman!

The language is different too. Gender neutral language is the norm and any deviation is strenuously challenged. Only the Tories oppose this, resolutely insisting on referring to 'Madam chairman' rather than 'chair' and groaning when language is challenged. Apart from the small handful of Welsh Conservatives, there is tangible evidence that for Assembly Members the generic use of 'he' to denote both sexes is language of the past. The Presiding Officer acts regularly to uphold the principle of gender neutral language. All documentation adheres to that principle except legislation which is governed by traditional statute from Westminster.

The Assembly has also deliberately adopted an informal style of address. There are few formal titles, apart from the Presiding Officer known as Llwydd. AMs address each other or Assembly Secretaries in the Chamber and Committees generally use first names. Again it is usually Tories who find this style discomforting and tend towards tradition and formality by using formal titles.

The determined approach to the use of language is important because it gives visible credence to the acknowledgement and valuing of difference. Since language inevitably reflects thinking and values, it marks out a very different discourse and political territory to the past overwhelming domination of Welsh politics by elderly, white men. Although the practice is respected and followed by Liberal Democrats and Nationalists, it is Labour that sets the tone and marks out the territory.

The topics and issues for debate are generally reflecting an agenda where women's influence is tangible and effective. Wales leads the UK with a Children's Commissioner with clear powers to protect and intervene on behalf of children. Health and social services dominate discussions. Money has been found for a Carers' strategy. Poverty and inequality are regular issues for debate. One of only two cross-cutting standing committees deals with Equal Opportunities. This has a responsibility for ensuring the mainstreaming of equalities issues across all subjects. It provides the opportunity for developing the programmes and measures that will give serious effect to the Assembly's statutory responsibility. Again, this places a seriousness and legitimacy on equality considerations in policy development and decision making which clearly challenges traditional procedures.

It is hard to judge how far this agenda is influenced by the presence of so many women and how much it is a reflection of the National Assembly's areas of competence – health, social services, housing, education, environment, economic development, arts and culture etc. Taking over the previous Welsh Office functions, the Assembly was always likely to impact on the services that make the difference to peoples' daily lives, services that women particularly care about.

Equally important in the challenge of creating a different politics is the style of debate. The aggression of politics, the endless point-scoring and confrontation so often hinders progress on the detail and clearly leads ordinary people, particularly women, to distrust politicians. It is an interesting and difficult question to judge the impact that so many women have on the knock-about of party politics, with the behind the scenes deals, political intrigue, competition and relentless jealousy.

Nancy Kline writes about women in leadership seeking ways of making work express their values. Referring to large corporations, she says, 'Personal values just do not come into the strategic plans... Male conditioning invented the corporation. And everything about it reflects the disconnected, defeat-to-win, control-as-you-lead, don't-be-too-different requirements of male conditioning.' (Kline 1993) If that is the case in American big business, it can be no less true of politics. For many men, the process seems more akin to a blood sport than the exercise in teambuilding, policy formation and action planning that the role of government might suggest to the uninitiated. And yet politics is a career which people enter specifically in order to express and further their values.

Changing men?

There is tangible evidence, certainly for me as a practised observer of gendered behaviour, that the presence of so many women, both in the Assembly generally and more specifically in the Labour group, also changes the behaviour of men. It gives legitimacy to those men that do want to work in a way that allows for co-operation and collaboration and places less emphasis on status and more on outcome. This is hard to judge in the maelstrom of politics and often hard to pin down with evidence.

Welsh politics has had much more than its fair share of drama, intrigue and deals as the process of devolution has progressed. The devolution referendum itself was a cliffhanger. Victory snatched from the jaws of defeat by the last result in the early hours of the morning clearly signalled the scepticism and uncertainty of Welsh people on greater self-government. It was the start of a roller coaster ride as Ron Davies was forced to resign as Labour leader, being replaced after another bitter struggle by Alun Michael. The legacy of resentment from the twinning battle was carried into the selections with several women facing hostility from local constituency parties mainly led by local men who felt 'passed over'. The impact of this aggressive atmosphere of control, anger and hostility was a serious set back for Labour and contributed to the poll result with a minority administration. Yet more potential for conflict, competition and aggression was unleashed as proportional representation freed the three other political parties from years of obscurity and marginalisation. In the Assembly's early months, despite the influence of women and the changed language and discourse, the Westminster style power play of some politicians was irresistible and significant. Ron Davies was forced to resign his position as a committee Chair. The Tory leader Rod Richards was forced to resign his position when charged with assault. There were votes of censure and no confidence, finally culminating in the resignation and subsequent return to Westminster of Alun Michael.

It is notable that men lead all four Welsh political parties and all four economic spokespeople are male. This has meant that men have dominated the most politically contentious of the debates, although it is hard to know what is cause and effect. Is it that the presence of men in those positions leads to the confrontational, point-scoring political challenges, feeding media interest and creating a momentum of their own? Would women in those positions operate in a similar manner? It is impossible to judge with any certainty but not unreasonable to hazard a guess. There is no question that the political activities of the male politicians are of significantly more interest to the (overwhelmingly male) political journalists. Television debates are most often comprised of three men and one woman. Gossip columns feature with much greater regularity the comings and goings of the male politicians. A full afternoon's debate on International Women's Day was notable for the fact that the press gallery was completely empty with virtually no media coverage or interest. The debate was lively, amusing, serious and moving, allowing women, and a reasonable number of men, to give serious thought to matters of major significance to over half the population of Wales. And yet overall men still speak more frequently in the Chamber. Women are less likely to intervene, speak for shorter periods and often admit to not needing to speak because others have already made their point – a factor that is rarely seen to inhibit a male politician!

There are encouraging signs that a higher degree of gender equality gives rise to serious, interesting and thoughtful debate in the Chamber and that this style of politics is valued by the electorate. There has been no evidence that voters are less likely to support women candidates. It is certainly the case that the Welsh electorate was keen to see a different style of politics. Many broke the habits of a lifetime by voting for a party other than Labour. Public opinion appears to favour more constructive debate, with political parties working together and a move away from yah-boo confrontations, which many see as evidence of immaturity, contributing to the failure of politicians to deal with deeply entrenched problems. Women are perceived with some apparent justification, as better able to focus on problem solving and less committed to point scoring.

Future aspirations

How does Labour's experience in Wales fit the New Labour philosophy? This is a hard question from a nation in which the Party, in seeking to define itself with a 'Welsh' rather than a 'Millbank' identity, now has a clear image as 'Welsh Labour' with all traces of 'new' discreetly hidden. And yet it is worth remembering that without the strong support from women members of the 'new' Labour National Executive Committee the great breakthrough created by twinning would not have taken place.

The process of achieving gender equality in political institutions is particularly important in its potential for the genuine empowerment of half the world's population. This means ensuring that women's aspirations are properly articulated and able to influence decision making by government. It is also the route by which we can develop the practical policies and programmes that will tackle the poverty and inequality so many women still struggle with on a daily basis. The experience in Wales, in my view, demonstrates that the case for equal representation is at the heart of genuine democracy because the inclusion and participation of women can change the agenda as well as the nature and outcome of political debate. If this is true of women who make up over half the population, it will also be true in relation to people excluded by virtue of race, disability and sexual orientation. This goes to the heart of the objectives of democratic socialism and is surely an aspiration for the 'Third Way'.

However, gender equality remains, and will be for the foreseeable future, fundamentally about power relations. To achieve change requires deliberate, planned intervention to redistribute the resources that give access to that power. Despite the very considerable progress made in the early days of our new Assembly, this is a fragile achievement in a tangled context of political institutions, workplaces and community ethos where gender difference is still a largely unwelcome and uncomfortable notion. We do not yet operate in a political environment where the style and agenda that women bring is able to flourish. Female politicians still cannot be assured of the seriousness and respect afforded to male politicians. If Labour, whatever its tag, is to pursue genuine equality of opportunity, much more must be done to support and accelerate the process of change.

Reference

Kline N (1993) *Women and Power* London: BBC Books

9. Women and the Scottish Parliament

Wendy Alexander

In 1876, Marion Bernstein, a music teacher in Glasgow, wrote about her hopes for Scottish women.

> I dreamt that the nineteenth century
> Had entirely passed away
> And had given place to a more advanced
> And very much brighter day.
>
> For Woman's Rights were established quite
> And man could the fact discern
> That he'd long been teaching his grandmama
> What she didn't require to learn.
>
> There were female chiefs in the Cabinet
> (Much better than males I'm sure)
> And the Commons were three parts feminine
> While the Lords were seen no more!
>
> And right well did the ladies legislate,
> They determined to keep the peace
> So well they managed affairs of State,
> That the science of war might cease.
>
> Now no man could venture to beat his wife,
> For the women had settled by law
> That whoever did so should lose his life,
> Then he'd never do so any more.
>
> There were no more physicians of either sex,
> For the schools were required to teach
> The science of healing to every child
> As well as the parts of speech.
>
> There were no more lawyers – all children learned
> The code of their country's laws;
> There were female judges, and truth became
> The fashion in every cause...

Marion Bernstein's dream still has to be realised. But the Scottish Parliament has brought it closer and her vision is a good standard by which to assess what has been achieved for Scottish women in the first year of its life.

'And the Commons were three parts feminine...'

In May 1999, 48 women took their seats as newly elected Members of the Scottish Parliament (MSPs) breaking all Scottish records for women's representation and more importantly bringing Scotland into line with countries such as Sweden and Norway, which topped the international league for women's representation.

Thirty-seven per cent of female MSPs falls well short of the 50:50 representation for which women activists campaigned. Nevertheless, it is a major step forward, substantially exceeding the 22 per cent women councillors elected on the same day, or the current 18 per cent representation rate for women at Westminster.

Such progress is not simply an accident. It would not have happened without the sustained efforts of many women across Scotland and beyond. The campaign was a response to Scotland's historically appalling record for returning women to Westminster and it culminated in the building of a consensus within Scottish Labour for a new approach to candidate selection for the new Parliament.

The case for equal representation was a significant debate in the Scottish Constitutional Convention and the subject of an Electoral Agreement between the two main political parties participating in the convention, Labour and the Liberal Democrats. In the end only the Scottish Labour Party operated a specific mechanism to achieve gender balance in representation. By twinning constituencies, Labour members selected a man and women to fight neighbouring constituencies. And the results speak for themselves; half of Labour's MSPs are women (King, 1993).

The Tories and the SNP, who had both opposed the Constitutional Convention, also opposed specific steps to increase women's representation in their selection systems. But while the Liberal Democrat's selection system failed to deliver, the power of moral suasion created by Labour's stance appears to have encouraged SNP activists to consider female candidates.

Gender composition of the Scottish Parliament

	Elected MSPs		Elected MSPs	
	Women	*Men*	*Women*	*Men*
	number of seats		*% of seats*	
Conservative	3	15	17	83
Labour	28	28	50	50
LibDems	2	15	12	88
SNP	15	20	43	57
Others	0	3	0	100
Totals	**48**	**81**	**37**	**63**

The twinning system has delivered for women and this should be the salient consideration when Scottish Labour decides – as it soon will – whether to maintain it in the future. Other challenges remain: no black MSP of any party has yet been elected to the Scottish Parliament.

'There were female chiefs in the Cabinet ...'

The additional member system of election for the Scottish Parliament introduced a much larger degree of proportionality than first-past-the-post. Consequently, no single party achieved an overall majority in the first Scottish Parliamentary elections in 1999. The Scottish Labour Party and the Scottish Liberal Democrats together have an overall majority and govern in coalition.

In selecting his administration of 22 ministers, the First Minister, Donald Dewar, appointed four Liberals and five women, all Labour. Three women – Sarah Boyack at Transport and Environment, Susan Deacon at Health, and myself at Communities – are in the Cabinet (making 27 per cent of the total). My Cabinet responsibilities include Equal Opportunities, but my colleague Jackie Baillie leads day to day on this key part of the portfolio. In the committee structure of the Parliament women chair six out of 16 (37 per cent). So overall women's voices are heard and there is a determination to 'let new politics breathe'.

The new politics should have policy and process dimensions. The process dimension is about how successful we have been in changing the culture of Scottish politics from old to new, masculine to feminine, destructive to constructive. But first let's look at the policy agenda. Because for Labour women, as for Marion Bernstein, equal representation should be a means to an end – that end being to improve the life chances of Scottish women.

'Right well did the ladies legislate...'

So what has the new Parliament done for Scottish women in its first year? Is it making a difference? The verdict must be that substantial progress has been made. The central commitments of the Labour-led administration are improving Scottish women's lives. Unemployment is at its lowest for a quarter of a century; hospital building is at an all time high; there are major school refurbishment plans and a determined assault on child poverty is underway: all address the core concerns of Scottish women. This is substantive political change, not just rhetoric. And Labour women, collectively determined to achieve outcomes, are content to experiment with innovative funding mechanisms if that is what it takes to reverse years of neglect in these essential policy areas.

But beyond the core commitments are specific policy developments that would not have come about had it not been for the presence of women, particularly Labour women, in the Scottish Parliament. Jackie Baillie and I have sought to reflect the concerns of those women at the heart of the Executive's programme. We have adopted an essentially two-tier approach: laying down long term foundations alongside immediate priorities for early action.

Into the long-term category fall things like setting up an Equality Unit, at the heart of the Executive, and bringing together work on race, disability, gender and on promoting equal opportunities. The Unit's initial work programme focuses on the mainstreaming of equalities issues into all policies and legislation, developing women friendly budgeting, and preparing a Scottish Equalities Strategy. Our determination to bring outside experts into the Unit, the political commitment of Executive colleagues and the support of parliamentary colleagues have all helped to pave the way for gender friendly policy making. Already we require a statement of potential impact on equal opportunities to accompany all Executive Bills.

And this sort of momentum means that concern about equalities is starting to influence a range of policies, from supporting women entrepreneurs and the national childcare strategy, to the reform of family law and public appointments systems. Cabinet colleagues, Susan Deacon at health and Sarah Boyack in transport are, respectively, tackling teenage sexual health and failures in cervical cancer screening, and examining women's experience of public transport.

'No man could venture to beat his wife...'

In addition to the long-term foundations, steps have been taken to tackle immediate injustices that have shamed us for too long. Above all we are determined to tackle domestic violence, or family crime as it is more appropriately known. We have set up the first ever multi-million pound national Anti-Domestic Abuse Fund that is already supporting 50 new projects across Scotland. These range from creating 100 extra refuge spaces and a national hotline, to training for health professionals to detect the early signs of abuse and piloting a national 'Respect' initiative in schools to make family crime abhorrent to our young people. We have listened to women's organisations, we have seconded skilled staff from Women's Aid and we are insisting that local authorities bid for these resources in partnership with women's organisations. The investment will be complemented by the recommendations of the Partnership on Domestic Violence, which will report shortly on the requisite changes to the criminal justice system in its treatment of such crimes. Women parliamentary colleagues have already made clear their impatience with the traditionally conservative approach of the Scottish criminal justice system, including the treatment of women testifying in rape trials.

'So well did they manage the affairs of state...'

The Scottish experience suggests that women make a difference not just through the issues that they champion, but in the way they approach mainstream services. Housing is just one example. We are proposing for Glasgow one of the most radical housing regeneration projects in Europe. Our plan is for community ownership, putting local people at the heart of neighbourhood renewal. It rejects the soulless bureaucracy of a distant housing department; it has no ideological prejudice against using private finance if it can lever in new investment; nor is it reluctant to tackle a sheltered direct service organisation that puts its own interests before those of the tenants it is meant to serve.

As Labour in Scotland has been wrestling with the legacies of municipal and community traditions in the provision of social housing – it has been Labour women, across the traditional left-right divide, who have championed the case for change, the community empowerment agenda and the idea that 'small is beautiful' in housing management. Next year we shall invite Glasgow's 90,000 council tenants to vote on proposals for change. Already half the politicians and many of the tenants on the management committee of the new Glasgow Housing Association (the new landlord) are women. This is a far cry from the male dominated corridors of the City Chambers.

So already Labour women in the Scottish Parliament are reaching out to the community and reviving strands of political activism that were championed by women in earlier generations but have long been forgotten or ignored. There are continuities between the rent strikers of yesteryear and our community-led investment plans for housing today. These include a recognition of the central role of women's leadership in those communities, and a willingness not to appropriate to any one political party the success of the community-based housing movement that, with female-dominated management committees, has helped to recreate working communities across Scotland over the last 25 years.

Women ministers, backed by parliamentary colleagues, are driving an agenda for change. Women parliamentarians have also championed issues such as childcare, the social economy, and equal pay – all important to women. The role of backbench MSPs, in particular through the powerful committee system, has been of fundamental importance. In Scotland's unicameral chamber the committees have taken on a role akin to the House of Lords at Westminster. Increasingly, once a powerful cross-party consensus has been achieved in committee, it is difficult to reverse it on the floor of the chamber. Time and again women parliamentarians have made their voices heard through the committees. For example, the support of three parliamentary committees for scrapping the notorious 'section 28' helped to hasten its repeal by 99 votes to 17. In the face of an overwhelmingly hostile press, women MSPs were prominent in ensuring that legislative safeguards applied to all children without distinctions based on the character of the parental relationship in the homes from which they came. Likewise, support in committee for the end to warrant sales is deeply rooted in Labour women's history and in their knowledge of what it is like trying to manage multiple household debts. And the reaction of Scottish MSPs to Mike Tyson wanting to fight in Glasgow can only be understood in terms of the revulsion felt by Scottish women that found an echo in their Parliament.

The contribution of women to shaping the Parliament's agenda has not been restricted to Labour. Roseanna Cunningham's stewardship of the Justice Committee has helped bring a feminist perspective to a range of criminal justice issues, ranging from the protection of rape victims at evidence sessions, to stronger action on stalking and harassment. So women from all parties have found the committee system a useful vehicle for making a difference. A desire for decisions rooted in women's experience is based on the testimonies heard in committee, rather than on any archaic procedures of an upper house that elsewhere has too often served to frustrate and obscure rather than to enlighten.

Scotland's experience echoes that of the Scandinavian countries: once a threshold of around 30 per cent is crossed for their share of seats, women can more easily influence the terms of debate. In particular, the numbers of women in the Labour group have helped to put issues on the agenda that would probably not have found favour with a more male dominated parliament. After barely a year, there is a long list of actions that would not have happened without the prominence of women MSPs, and the critical factor has often been the force of backbench parliamentary colleagues urging Executive action.

'What she did not require to learn...'

But what of the process, the much sought-after 'new politics' that the Scottish Parliament was supposed to hasten? In many ways the evolution of the committee system over the last year has fulfilled the ambitions of the Consultative Steering Group (CSG) that drew up the working arrangements for the Parliament. The powerful women on the CSG were particularly determined that Westminster-style debates should stay at Westminster.

Contrary to the pessimism of some commentators, I think the CSG's vision, built on the principles of power-sharing, accountability, access, participation, and equal opportunities is triumphing because women parliamentarians, in particular, want it to work. There are risks in generalising, but the Scottish experience suggests the women are more concerned with outcomes than with rhetoric. In other words, what counts most to women is what they do rather than what they say. A relative lack of interest in the cut and thrust of debate for its own sake, coupled with a deep emotional commitment to 'doing the right thing' (as they see it) is powerfully felt by most Labour women. But we live in an age when the politics of perception rather than the politics of outcomes dominates the news pages.

Spin, splits and 'stooshies', to use a good Scots word, is the stuff of the media circus that reports politics these days. The Scottish Parliamentary lobby (overwhelmingly male) sometimes seems to think it knows the rules better than the politicians. And it has precious little time for politicians who might want to change the rules. All Scottish editors (including the first-ever woman, recently appointed) and sub editors learned their trade in the Westminster school, where debating prowess, tribal loyalties and standoffs between governments and backbenchers are most highly valued. By contrast the politics of consensus seeking, committee testimony and making common cause may be judged dull and lifeless. Which perspective wins the day will determine a lot about the politics of the new Scotland.

'And truth became the fashion in every cause...'

Will a new politics survive? Frankly it is too early to say. But there are Labour women who will give their political lives to keep up the momentum for change. There are challenges for both process and policy. On process, women do not want to play by the old rules. Our family friendly working practices, although far from perfect, are an advance on many other legislatures, and having so many parliamentary allies (both male and female) in the cause of change gives new approaches a fighting chance, despite the cynicism of the media, some male colleagues and too many public servants. The procedures of the Scottish Parliament are our ally as we try to resist defaulting to the Westminster model that we all know too well.

On policy perhaps the pre-eminent challenge in Scotland, as in the rest of the UK, is around issues of work-life balance. This complex agenda is one where we can only make progress in partnership with Westminster. Similarly we have a common agenda across the UK around tackling exclusion. Women's exclusion is often invisible, yet many women continue to be barred from full participation because of their lower incomes, patterns of working and caring or domestic responsibilities, and because of enduring discriminatory assumptions about their role and place in society.

Scottish politics continues to be coloured by the constitutional question and so the perspectives of women on the worth of the Westminster connection will be of vital importance. If Scottish women believe that the only way we can end child poverty is by working, not warring, with Westminster, the United Kingdom is safe.

Women care about the issues that touch their families. They aspire for themselves and for their children. So the party that owns the future by offering hope will not be one that continues to claim that where you were born is more important than what you believe. There are tough debates that women, for too long marginalized, now want to be at the heart of – for example, how in this century do we combine a commitment to tolerance and diversity in our society with a renewed commitment to community? These are the issues on which the Scottish Parliament must speak with fresh voices.

'...a more advanced and very much brighter day.'

My colleague Sarah Boyack said: 'I think Labour has responded to the feminist agenda, but we still have some way to go in changing the culture, we still have to work on it within the party.' If the legacy of feminism, as Lynne Segal has suggested, lies in its striving to 'keep relating the personal and cultural to the economic and political, however forbidding and precarious that enterprise may be', then Scottish women in the Parliament and beyond are hard at work (Segal, 1999). In summing up the Scottish challenge, which doubtless has wider echoes, Joyce McMillan wrote of the need to avoid that 'wild pendulum swing back towards more traditional roles by learning how to integrate the values we once called womanly into the public world we inhabit... We have had a feminist century; when women have begun to show that they can do all that men can. But now we need to move on together towards more womanly times, in which men and women alike will have both the freedom to achieve to the height of their abilities, and the time to live well and wisely in between'(McMillan, 2000).

Women in the Parliament have stood on their mother's shoulders and made a promising start. But progress always depends on learning as well as leading. We need to find more effective ways of engaging with Scottish women and working with colleagues across the UK and elsewhere if we are to realise Marion Bernstein's vision. We already have a 'very much brighter day' but if Marion were around I suspect she would urge us to right old wrongs and meet new challenges.

References

King E (1993) *The Hidden History of Glasgow's Women: the new factor* Edinburgh: Mainstream Publishing

McMillan J (2000) 'Is this the dawning of the age of the female?' *The Scotsman* 1.1.00

Segal L (1999) *Why Feminism?* Oxford: Polity Press

10. Quality and equality on the council: renewing local democracy

Mary-Ann Stephenson

I've worked with male councillors for thirty odd years and I have never once heard a male councillor say he had to go home to get the kids tea, or pick up the kids from school.
Liberal Democrat male councillor

The reform of local government is an important part of the Government's programme to reform and modernise our democratic institutions. Such reform is long overdue. While voter turn out in general is falling, turn out in local elections is particularly low. The average turn out in May 2000 was 32 per cent. This appears to be linked to a lack of faith in local government to deliver for voters. As Matthew Taylor points out in a paper for the Local Government Association, the 1999 British Social Attitudes Survey reported that only 35 per cent of voters trusted their local councillors to make decisions about local issues, compared with 64 per cent who would trust a 'jury' of their fellow citizens (Taylor, 2000).

Reform of local government should be particularly important to women. Local government is responsible for decisions on local education, housing and social services, all of which are of crucial concern to women. Many of the new Government policies that are likely to affect women's lives will be implemented at a local level, including the national childcare strategy, the new deal for communities and policies to tackle domestic violence.

But women remain severely under-represented in local government. On a national average, only one in four councillors is a woman. In some local authorities, such as Bolsover, Durham and Anglesea, the numbers fall below one in ten. Turnover among women councillors is high, with many lasting only one or two terms before resigning. Women are acutely under-represented at senior levels in local government as council leaders or chairs of powerful committees. Unless this situation is resolved the democratic legitimacy of the new local authority structures, such as cabinet style government, will be called into question. Local authority cabinets are likely to be formed by the same people who currently hold positions as committee chairs. A cabinet that is entirely or largely dominated by men is unlikely to be seen as representative by the majority of women voters.

The reasons behind the lack of women on local councils are inextricably linked with the other problems of local government. Research by the Fawcett Society published in June 2000 suggests that the assumptions and behaviour of many local councillors say as much about why local government is unpopular among voters as why there are so few women elected (Gill, 2000). And the reforms needed to make local government attractive and open to women could hold the key to many of the other problems faced by local government.

What puts women off?

Explanations for the lack of women in elected institutions fall into three separate but strongly linked categories: factors that put women off standing, practical barriers that make it difficult to stand and discrimination at the point of selection or election.

At Westminster, women MPs have identified discrimination by selection committees as the main barrier to women's representation, closely followed by practical problems created by working hours and a political culture that is not woman friendly (Fawcett Society, 1997). Most women MPs agree on the need to change the culture of politics, which creates barriers for women at every stage. Women may decide against standing for office because they dislike the political culture that excludes them. A culture dominated by men may create practical barriers for women if it does not take account of women's caring responsibilities when agreeing working hours. And the culture within selection committees may lead to assumptions about the ability of women candidates, or their attractiveness to the electorate that result in discriminatory practices at selection.

The strategy of all-women shortlists adopted by Labour in the run up to the 1997 General Election not only aimed to counter the discrimination women faced. It was also part of an attempt to change the male dominated political culture of Westminster by creating a critical mass of women MPs. All-women shortlists cut through the chicken and egg problem of how to change a male dominated culture when it served to exclude the very women who might change it. This was possible at Westminster level because, despite a political environment that put many women off standing, there was still no shortage of able potential women candidates.

The same is not true of local government. Although women councillors interviewed by Fawcett complained of discrimination within their parties, most said the real problem was finding anyone, woman or man, who was willing to stand as a councillor at all. Many talked of the need for 'arm twisting' to find anyone who would be willing to represent the party in their ward. Of the councillors interviewed, several had not been a member of any party, and had only thought of standing for the council after they had been approached by a party member. One councillor told how an approach by the Liberal Democrats made her consider standing as a councillor, although when she did stand it was as an independent.

Several councillors complained of the poor calibre of candidates their party was forced to accept. One councillor interviewed in April 2000 said:

If the political parties, let alone the public, had a full choice as to who they would put forward there are probably at least half a dozen people on the council who would not have been selected. (Labour, male)

Without a pool of willing candidates to call on in many parts of the country, the sort of positive action mechanisms that worked so well in the 1997 General Election and in Scotland and Wales in 1999 are likely to be far less effective.

The most obvious reason for the lack of candidates willing to stand is the difficulty of combining council work with a paid job, and family responsibilities. This is particularly difficult for women who still bear the main burden of caring work within families.

Tonight is the fourth night this week that I am out. Me and my husband get quality time on Saturday and Sunday night, and that's when I'm asleep. (Labour, female)

You know it is not easy when you are a working mum, if you are not there at that vital time between four and six. So what do we do? We have council meetings that start at four. And why do we start at four? Because it was more convenient for the men. (Lib Dem, male)

With an increasingly long hours culture for those in paid work, the working day can extend into the evening when council meetings are held. For women with children or other caring responsibilities early evening is precisely the time when they are preparing meals, supervising homework and getting young children to bed. For many, council work can only be considered after retirement. Not surprisingly the average age of local councillors is 54.8 for women and 55 for men and around a third of local councillors are retired.

As fewer people have time to devote to local council work, parties can find it difficult to select good candidates. The need to find somebody, anybody, to stand in some wards in turn reflects on the reputation of the council, as one Labour councillor described:

We have had one or two councillors in the past couple of years who have struggled. The party was desperate to get people to stand in seats and they got elected. They had no political philosophy, they had little understanding of how the Labour party worked, let alone how they interacted with Government and local government and they really did struggle. They ended up isolated and victimised and felt they weren't being involved when in fact they just couldn't handle the amount of information they were being given.

> They were not an advert for local government, or the Labour party or anything. We did them no favours and vice versa. (Labour, male)

Better training and support for new councillors might help overcome some of these problems but unless parties can encourage and enable more potential councillors to come forward they will always have to select from a limited pool.

Culture of complacency

The changes needed to make this happen are unlikely while there is still such a widespread culture of complacency among many councillors. Because while most women councillors appeared to recognise the problems that prevented most other women standing, many of their male colleagues do not, as the following exerpts from Fawcett's interviews with male councillors suggest:

> People say they haven't got the time which is a load of rubbish because folk always make time for the things they want to do so it's just an excuse. (Lib Dem, male)

> I can't remember any of the girls ever being late for a meeting. They all have grown up families and are in their late forties, early fifties. None of them have ever said to me 'this [the timing of meetings] is ridiculous'. (Independent, male)

> I suppose the timing of meetings may deter some prospective councillors from coming forward, I don't know I haven't come across that. (Lib Dem, male)

These attitudes may be more prevalent among older councillors, some of whom have served on the council for twenty or thirty years and are clearly happy with the status quo. While complaining about the lack of suitable candidates, they did not acknowledge that there was anything they could do that might improve matters:

> If you are interested enough you will do it anyway, like myself...

> I couldn't put my finger on why people are not interested. I know in the past I have had difficulty getting people to stand. (Lib Dem, male)

For these councillors the blame could be placed squarely on the shoulders of those who did not come forward, and the reason they did not come forward was the same reason few people voted – apathy. Describing voters as apathetic offers a convenient excuse for those who do not wish to change the way political institutions operate. In this analysis women and younger people don't get involved in the council because they are not particularly interested. Voters do not turn out because they can't be bothered. The council works well for those 'who are interested enough' but has no responsibility to engage anyone else.

> I don't think antipathy to local government can be reversed or addressed, because the means of correcting it are beyond our powers (Lib Dem, male)

Getting engaged

Women are particularly likely to be described as apathetic, in keeping with a widely held view that women are less interested in politics than men. However, research by Fawcett and others has suggested that women care deeply about a wide range of political issues. They are simply less likely to engage with a political culture that excludes them. So long as political discourse remains dominated by men the issues considered 'political' and the language used to debate them may fail to resonate with women voters. Women interviewed in recent Fawcett focus groups tended to be dismissive when asked what they thought about politics, but talked at length about pensions and welfare benefits, housing, health, education, the environment and the problems they faced balancing work with caring responsibilities. Those who were most active in formal and informal voluntary and community groups tended to see the council as at best an irrelevance and at worst a barrier to what they were trying to achieve.

Developing improved links with voluntary and community groups can be an important way to build links between the issues that engage women voters and the politics of the council. Pam Giddy argues that there is a strong link between the presence of women on a local council and the existence of a robust network of community groups focussing on and run by women (Giddy, 2000). Without women councillors to support, encourage, and argue for funding for these groups and projects, they are less likely to survive.

While many councillors work hard to create formal alliances and informal links with these voluntary groups, others appear not to notice that they exist. In areas where the same party has dominated the council for thirty or forty years there is little need for councillors to engage with voters in order to keep their place on the council. In 1997-8 one in five local authorities in Great Britain was dominated by one party that held at least 80 per cent of the seats. In 22 of these councils there was an opposition of just two or three councillors (Giddy, 2000). These councils often see little turnover of councillors from one year to the next, so that the council is still dominated by people who won their seats in the early 1970s. Under the first-past-the-post electoral system it is unlikely that these councillors will ever risk losing their seats, which makes it relatively easy for them to lose touch with local voters. Voters are less likely to turn out to vote if they think politicians have lost touch with their concerns, or that their vote will not make a difference. In the local elections in May 2000 some of the safest Labour councils saw the turn-out drop to below 20 per cent of the electorate. Low turn-out cannot simply be blamed on voter apathy; it is at least partly the result of the complacency of councillors who do not believe that they are in any way responsible for a diminishing engagement with politics.

Low turnover among (predominantly male) councillors not only encourages complacency. When seats rarely come up for election there are few opportunities for women to get elected. Ending single party rule by changing the voting system to a system of proportional representation could be an important step towards opening up local government to women.

However, a change in the voting system alone will not be enough to encourage more candidates to stand for election. Finding the time for council work is difficult for women in particular as they already struggle to combine paid work with the main responsibility for caring within families. While some councillors have called for employers to allow time off for council duties during the day, this is unlikely to be an option for many people. Small employers will find it difficult to give staff the amount of time off that local government requires. Even if employees were given the legal right to time off for council work it is likely, as with the right not to work more than 48 hours a week, that they would find they could only exercise the right at the expense of their career. So long as being a councillor is a voluntary post it will be difficult to design working hours that are family friendly.

Paying the price

Westminster politics still suffers from the legacy of a time when national politics was a voluntary activity. MPs were expected to spend the day in the city or in court, popping along to Parliament for dinner and a spot of legislation later in the day. The working hours of Westminster have yet to move on from this model. However the concept of an MP's role as essentially voluntary no longer exists. Democratic reformers recognised that it was essential to pay MPs if national politics were to be opened up to those without a private income. Opening up local government to a wider range of people may require similar steps. Paying a full time salary would be expensive, unless the number of local councillors was reduced. Alternatively council work could be recognised, and paid as a part-time job, making it particularly attractive to women with caring responsibilities.

Some councillors already treat their work as a full-time job, giving up paid work and surviving on expenses. However, payment of expenses varies from council to council. Expenses paid for attendance at meetings encourage meetings to be valued at the expense of other council work. The term 'expenses' also encourages the feeling among voters that councillors are corrupt, only in politics for the financial benefits it brings. Paying councillors a salary might face resistance from voters who have little confidence in local government, but the changes needed to re-build that confidence are unlikely to happen unless many more people – and many more kinds of people – are encouraged to enter local politics.

The process of democratic renewal held out by the Government's programme of reform for local government will not be realised if the personnel and attitudes remain unchanged. Reform cannot simply be limited to re-organising institutions, or creating new ones as in Scotland and Wales. It must also involve changing the culture of those institutions. From early on in the Scottish Constitutional Convention it was recognised that a Scottish Parliament would have little legitimacy if it failed properly to represent the people of Scotland. The same is true of local government. Only a local democracy that truly reflects society as a whole is likely to re-engage voters.

References

Fawcett Society (1997) *Survey of Women MPs* London: Fawcett.

Giddy P (2000) *A Woman's Place is in the Chamber* London: Local Government Association.

Gill B (2000) *Losing Out Locally* London: Fawcett.

Taylor M (2000) *Changing Political Culture* London: Local Government Association.

III: Work and Family
– getting it right

11. Juggling with reciprocity: towards a better balance
Stuart White and Diane Gardner

As public philosophy and political practice, social democracy is distinguished by its commitment to, and expansive conception of, social rights: rights of access, indeed of equal access, to important social goods such as education, health-care, and a decent income. Of late, however, social democratic politicians have been at pains to emphasize that social democracy is about more than rights. It is also, they repeat, about responsibilities. The holder of social rights has responsibilities to society that he/she must perform in return for the rights and opportunities that society provides. Indeed, enjoyment of the social goods that are the subject of these rights ought in some cases to be strictly conditional on the citizen meeting these responsibilities. Contemporary social democracy thus centres on an explicit politics of civic reciprocity.

A politics of civic reciprocity ought not to be seen as an alternative to a politics of equality (as social democratic politics is traditionally conceived). Rather, civic reciprocity has a legitimate and important place within a politics of equality. Nevertheless, the relationship between the two needs to be thought through with some care. Critics may have a point when they allege that social democracy has in the past pursued equality in ways that were insufficiently attentive to the demands of civic reciprocity. But we need to be aware of the opposite danger as well: that the demands of civic reciprocity (the responsibilities it is thought to entail) may be conceptualized, and subsequently enforced, in ways that reinforce or exacerbate unjust inequalities.

One worry, for example, is that an ill-conceived politics of civic reciprocity will reinforce inequalities based on class. Workfare and related programmes will ensure that the poor meet their supposed productive responsibilities. But such schemes arguably do little to ensure that the rich are satisfying their equivalent responsibilities. The burdens of reciprocity then fall with inequitable heaviness on the shoulders of the least well-off. Another worry (though by no means entirely separable from the first) is that an ill-conceived politics of civic reciprocity will reinforce gender-based inequality. In particular, the prevailing conception of responsible citizenship accords pride of place to work (to such an extent that civic reciprocity is often equated with a new 'work ethic'). But what kinds of work ought to count as satisfying the legitimate demands of civic reciprocity? How, more specifically, should we incorporate the (typically unpaid) work of parents and other carers into a public conception of civic reciprocity? The way we answer such questions has a very important bearing on how the politics of civic reciprocity affects the goal of gender equality and, indeed, the well-being of society as a whole.

Underpinning equal citizenship

Economic justice is widely thought to require respect for a principle of reciprocity, according to which: *those who willingly share in the social product ought, if possible, to make a productive contribution to the community in return*. Our society can be conceived ideally as a commonwealth, an association for cooperative provision of the resources which, as individuals and households, we will selectively draw upon in pursuing our respective visions of the good life. If economic cooperation is to be fair then the rules governing the distribution of the social product must give some weight to the idea of mutual advantage. If, through one's claims on the social product, one benefits from the industry of other members of the commonwealth, then, so far as one can, given one's relative capacities, one ought to try to ensure that others similarly benefit from your membership. One ought to 'do one's bit' in this sense. Other citizens have a right to expect this of you. How could one simply refuse such a duty without thereby implying that one's fellow citizens exist for one's own convenience, and without thus asserting an aristocratic relationship to them that contradicts the basic ethos of equal citizenship? Far from being in- or anti-egalitarian, the principle of reciprocity may be regarded as one expression of the ethic of mutual respect on which egalitarianism rests. For this reason, the reciprocity principle seems to be of intrinsic importance.

Respect for reciprocity is also instrumentally important, however, insofar as obvious violations of the reciprocity principle will undermine the legitimacy of economic arrangements and, thus, the willingness of individuals to maintain these arrangements. This is perhaps especially true of egalitarian arrangements which involve significant amounts of redistribution. If egalitarian objectives are pursued in a way that is inattentive to economic free-riding and parasitism, there is a clear risk that the egalitarian institutions in question will provoke feelings of alienation and resentment and so undercut the very spirit of solidarity on which they depend. In this vein, Samuel Bowles and Herbert Gintis have recently argued that popular resistance to the American welfare state derives not from an opposition to egalitarian redistribution per se, but to redistribution that enables citizens to evade the contributive responsibilities that derive from a widely shared norm of 'strong reciprocity' (Bowles and Gintis, 1998-9, pp4-10). They start with the observation, confirmed in a variety of experimental settings, that individuals tend not to conform to the standard model of 'homo economicus' who rationally pursues his/her self-interest without regard to any norms of fairness. But nor are people unconditional altruists. Rather, they tend to be *conditional* cooperators, willing to do their bit in cooperative ventures to which they belong so long as they can be assured that others will also make a reasonable contribution: 'homo reciprocans'. Widespread adherence to the norm may be explicable in evolutionary terms: communities in which homo reciprocans predominates may find it easier to solve important problems of trust and collective action than communities in which homo economicus predominates. If, however, commitment to the reciprocity norm is deep-rooted, then egalitarians must frame their reform proposals in a way that explicitly acknowledges and upholds the norm of reciprocity rather than being indifferent to it.

Tradition and the market

In accordance with the reciprocity principle, we might stipulate that all citizens who enjoy access to a specified (and high) minimum of the social product, embodied in various 'social rights', have a corresponding obligation to make a suitably specified minimum productive contribution to the community. As it stands, however, this statement of the reciprocity principle is obviously very abstract. To make it more concrete we need to say more about what sort of things might properly count as forms of 'contribution' in satisfaction of the principle. To simplify the question for present purposes: what kinds of work ought to count in satisfaction of this principle? Various conceptions of civic reciprocity can be distinguished by the way in which they answer this question.

One response to the foregoing question is as follows: men (husbands) may and should satisfy the reciprocity principle primarily through paid employment, while women (wives) may and should satisfy it primarily through domestic care work (which is typically unwaged). This conception of civic reciprocity rests on a number of assumptions. One assumption is that citizens naturally sort themselves into male-female couples through marriage. A second is that there is a natural division of labour within these couples in which the male partner focuses on paid work in the formal economy while the female partner specializes in unwaged care work within the home. Both kinds of work are then given some acknowledgement as forms of productive contribution satisfying the demands of civic reciprocity, though not necessarily as contributions carrying equal entitlement to public benefits. William Beveridge's war-time report, Social Insurance and Allied Services, seems to be based on something akin to this traditional conception of civic reciprocity (Beveridge, 1942). Commitment to this conception of civic reciprocity has also been a feature of Christian Democratic ideology in continental Europe and its influence in these countries is still reflected in the male-breadwinner assumptions underpinning their welfare states and, relatedly, in their relatively low rates of female labour force participation (Esping-Andersen, 1990).

What if the breadwinning father-husband in the Beveridgian/Christian Democratic couple disappears? Here, the traditional conception holds that the wife-mother ought not to go out to work but ought to concentrate on the provision of care within the home. In the words of the social democratic theorist, Leonard Hobhouse, writing in 1911: 'if we take in earnest all that we say of the rights and duties of motherhood, we shall recognise that the mother of young children is often doing better service to the community and one more worthy of pecuniary remuneration when she stays at home and minds her children than when she goes out charing and leaves them to the chances of the street or to the perfunctory care of a neighbour'(Hobhouse, 1993, p87). This conception of civic reciprocity was quite consistent, therefore, with payment of welfare benefits to single mothers without any test of willingness to work (in the sense of taking paid employment). It is important to stress, however, that this did not reflect a view that single parent families were legitimate *per se*. The working assumption was that the single parent family was, as it were, a 'damaged two-person household': the real breadwinning father and husband had died or irresponsibly abandoned his family, making it necessary for the state to step in as a surrogate breadwinning father-husband. Similar assumptions underpinned the introduction of Aid to Dependent Children in the US under President Franklin Roosevelt's New Deal.

Since the eras of Hobhouse, Roosevelt and Beveridge, the participation of women in the labour market has increased significantly. This has in large part reflected women's (imperfect) emancipation from the confinement implied by the Beveridgian household, and their assertion and pursuit of a right to equal life-chances with men. Changes in family structure have interacted with women's entry into the labour force, as both effect and further cause. In some countries, such as the US, pressure to enter the labour force, and to work longer hours, may have increased as a result of a depression in wage rates among lower earners, perhaps also due to more intense intra-firm competition among professionals to display commitment through long hours in the office, and by the connection of elements of the social wage (for example, health-care) to employment (Burtless, 1999, pp18-22)[1]. In the US case, welfare reform has added to this pressure to work, by increasing pressure on low-income single parents to enter the workforce (Sawhill, 1999, p28).

The interest in welfare reform is indicative, however, of how perceptions of what civic reciprocity rightfully demands of us can change with the growth in women's employment. This growth has had as its corollary some weakening of the assumption that a women's place is properly and primarily in the home. But if this Beveridgian assumption is put in doubt, what are we, as a society, to make of those women who, as Hobhouse proposed, stay at home and look after their children at the public expense? For many people, the thought arises: should these women not also, to some extent, be out there in the labour market doing what they reasonably can to earn their living? In particular, if mothers in two-parent familes are no longer confined to the home, are properly active in the labour market, shouldn't single mothers be working in jobs to some significant extent as well? In 1911 Hobhouse found it obvious that paying single mothers to stay at home and raise their children is fully consistent with the principle that income should follow productive service. However, by the 1990s in the US, single mothers doing precisely this had come to be seen as the very model of unproductive, non-reciprocating parasitism (Quandagno, 1994). Hence the demand for 'welfare reform' that would put an end to this perceived parasitism by requiring single parents to seek and take employment. Thus, as the traditional assumptions about women's proper place in the division of labour have weakened, an alternative market-based conception of civic reciprocity has begun to emerge, a conception which identifies real productive contribution reductively with paid employment.

As intimated, this development is perhaps most pronounced in the US. As the dominant conception of civic reciprocity there becomes increasingly market-based, domestic and family care work is seen less and less as an aspect of citizenship and more and more as a purely private concern. As Mona Harrington puts it: 'The reigning idea is not at all complicated: the private family is responsible for family care and should provide it through its own resources' (Harrington, 1999; p30). Pushing this way of looking at the world to an extreme, the decision to have a child (or to look after an infirm elderly relative) can be conceptualized simply as one kind of life-style choice on a par with, say, a decision to pursue an interest in bungee-jumping or mountain-climbing. No citizen can credibly claim public subsidy or special regulations to secure time off work to help him or her pursue a lively interest in bungee-jumping or mountain-climbing. Thus, following the argument to its logical conclusion, no citizen can legitimately expect public subsidy or rights to time off work as a parent or carer. The Clinton administrations have fought this philosophy to some extent – the introduction of a right to unpaid family leave was the first major item of legislation enacted in Bill Clinton's first term – but it remains immensely powerful.

There are some things to be said for the market-based conception of civic reciprocity as an alternative to the traditional conception. Most obviously, it does not rely on the same questionable assumptions about women's proper place in society and the home. But it is also objectionable on a number of grounds. It is an obvious point, but one that has perhaps come to need underlining, that societies like Britain and the US do not rely solely on the market for their material reproduction. In addition to a highly developed system of production of goods and services coordinated through the market there is also (and is likely to remain) a system of production based around the family and the home. It seems implausible and unfair, on the face of it, to deny contributive status to work of the latter kind by conceptualizing civic reciprocity in purely market-based terms – a tendency which some have perceived in recent attempts to delineate a 'Third Way' public philosophy (Sevenhuijsen, 1999). For example, the wider community has an obvious interest in the welfare and character of its future citizens and, therefore, in the proper nurturance and support of its children. Those who perform the work of caring for children thereby take upon themselves a definite share of publicly valuable labour, labour which is thus reasonably seen as at least partly satisfying the contributive obligation these individuals have under the reciprocity principle.[2] If, in addition, we accept that there is a social, community-wide obligation to provide support for the disabled or infirm elderly, then those who take upon themselves the task of caring for disabled or infirm elderly relatives are thereby taking upon themselves what is, morally speaking, a shared burden. Other citizens owe them something in return for their willingness to shoulder a burden which, in a moral sense, belongs to us all. Though such work may be done in a 'private' sphere, and may not be paid for by its beneficiaries, it can and generally does have a public value.

Aside from its inherent unfairness, however, a drift in the direction of a reductively market-based conception of civic reciprocity ignores, and threatens to exacerbate, a number of problems that stem from the increasing difficulty that familes currently face in trying to integrate the demands of employment and care. The present situation carries considerable risks, firstly, for gender equality. To a very considerable extent, women are still expected to be primary care givers, in accordance with the Beveridgian model of the household, at the same time as they are both seeking and coming under pressure to do more paid work. It is, in consequence, women who are most vulnerable to the strains of trying to reconcile the competing demands of care work and employment. This is inequitable in itself and is likely to undermine genuine equality of opportunity between men and women in the workplace (Harrington, 1999; p17).

In addition, there may be significant negative externalities to society at large from this situation. Society suffers, for example, if skilled and energetic people are effectively forced out of employment because of the difficulty of balancing employment and care (Wilson, 2000). Alternatively, individuals may respond to the potential 'time squeeze' by avoiding care responsibilities in the first place, eg, by choosing to have fewer or no children. There is some evidence that this is how many couples in the US have responded in recent years to the difficulties of balancing employment and parenthood (Burtless, 1999). There is perhaps an argument to be had about whether declining fertility rates in advanced capitalist countries are, in the global scheme of things, a good or bad development. But declining fertility rates may pose a problem within these societies themselves by accentuating problems of population ageing which are thought to threaten the long-term viability of the welfare state (Esping-Andersen, 1999, pp170-84).

Civic reciprocity: a better balance

We conclude that liberal capitalist societies like Britain and the US need to find a more balanced relationship between market-based employment activity and the demands of care work. Relatedly, these societies need a new conception of civic reciprocity that will reflect and help consolidate this new balance between employment and care. For want of a better term we shall refer to this as the integrated conception of civic reciprocity (because it aims at a happier integration of participation in the market and performance of care responsibilities). The integrated conception calls for the public acknowledgement of contributive status of care work. Concretely, this would involve clarifying and seeking to enact three sets of obligations:

- *Employer obligations to support care responsibilities.* Employers have an obligation to make terms and conditions of employment more attuned to the demands of family life and responsibilities of care. To some extent, this obligation may and should be enforced directly through legislation, eg, to establish rights to parental leave and, perhaps, to hold one's existing job on a part-time basis for a period of time following the birth of a child. Beyond this, the government might also offer firms tax incentives to encourage experimentation with new work processes that give individual employees more flexibility in allocating their time between the workplace and the family (Harrington, 1999, pp52-3).

- *Community-wide obligations to support care responsibilities.* It is neither feasible nor fair to place the full burden of support for care responsibilities on the shoulders of employers. This does not mean that the remaining weight has to fall only on the individual and family, however. Rather, we must share the burden out across the community. In this vein, policy needs more emphatically to embrace and develop the idea of what we might call the *carer's wage*: the social wage paid to those who perform publicly valuable care work. This social wage might take various forms and have several components, including refundable tax credits for parents and other carers, similar credits for child care, and a right to paid parental leave (Kelly, 1999). In determining the precise level of the carer's wage, the community will of necessity have to address the question of what level of labour market participation it can reasonably demand of different types of carers (such as single parents), and we would stress the importance of answering this question through a process that is genuinely public and democratic, giving all affected parties fair opportunity to advance their views (Gutmann and Thompson, 1996, pp303-6; Fraser, 1989, pp144-160).

- *Individuals' obligations to offer good care.* Individual carers themselves have a civic obligation to offer good quality care. A key issue here is that of carer capacity, by which we mean the bundle of competencies individuals require to perform their caring responsibilities well. Traditionally the state has assumed that parents have adequate capacity as carers and has intervened only in extreme situations to rescue children from abusive parents. But, given how important the first years of life are for child development, there may also be a role here for more preventive policy aimed at building parental capacities.

How will this alternative politics of civic reciprocity affect the goal of gender equality? A critic might argue as follows: women will likely make much greater use than men of generous subsidies for care work to limit labour market participation; in this way, these subsidies will serve to reinforce the existing gendered division of labour according to which care work is properly women's work. Some blow for gender equality.

This criticism seems harsh when the proposed approach is judged against the market-based alternative. Relative to that alternative, this approach would alleviate the situation of many women who are presently struggling to combine employment and family life. It would make it easier for some women to maintain some participation in the labour market even while adopting the primary care role within the family. Given that there is a gendered division of labour in our society, which is not going to disappear very soon, the proposed approach surely protects and advances women's interests better than the market-based alternative.

Nevertheless, if the ultimate goal is a 'humanist' society (Moller Okin, 1989), in which there are no distinct spheres of specifically 'men's work' or 'women's work', then this criticism ought to worry us. It suggests that a new politics of civic reciprocity is hardly, by itself, sufficient for this end. However, we presumably do not want the state to enforce an equal division of care work between men and women. For there are, and probably always will be, perfectly legitimate differences between individuals, regardless of gender, in enthusiasm for such work, and we do not want a society in which parents may not make decisions about the division of care work for themselves to match their preferences. The state's role properly consists in ensuring that these decisions do reflect genuine choices, and (relatedly, but a little more strongly) that they are made against a background of genuine equality of opportunity between men and women. Securing these conditions carries us into the whole mainstream of public policy: into education, training, health-care, pensions, as well as the areas of social welfare touched upon briefly above. Across this wide range of policy, we have to ask what messages we are sending as a community – perhaps quite unconsciously – about the role of women (and men) in society; and we have to identify the social obstacles that particularly obstruct women in adopting new roles on a footing of equality with men. Many aspects of this agenda are explored elsewhere in this book.

Finally, we have to remember that feminism – the relatively organized, self-conscious expression of gender equity politics – is in many ways a politics that works directly on the terrain of civil society, of national-popular culture, and not only through the agencies of the state. But changes in state policy can create a springboard for new initiatives within civil society. And a new politics of civic reciprocity, centred on a public revaluation of, and support for, care work, perhaps provides an excellent opportunity to renew and deepen popular discussion about the status of care work in men's, as well as women's, lives.

The authors wish to thank the editor of this volume and Susan Giaimo for comments and helpful conversation on this topic.

Endnotes

1   Average hours worked per week increased most markedly amongst women in the second and third quintiles of the income distribution between 1968 and 1998, perhaps a response to real wage stagnation amongst lower-paid workers in the US over this period (though women's hourly wages have increased in the past 20 years). It is still women in the top quintile, however, who work the most hours per week on average of all women, perhaps reflecting the competitive pressures of professional employment.

2   At the very least, care work of this kind must have a presumption of contributive status under the reciprocity principle, though, as a matter of philosophical consistency, we would concede that not all such work is necessarily contributive in this sense since, in some circumstances, having more than a certain number of children might constitute a public bad for the society in question. However, even in these circumstances, we would be wary of letting the full costs of child-raising fall on parents unless the society in question has gone a considerable way towards eliminating unjust background inequalities in access to income and wealth.

References

Beveridge W (1942) *Social Insurance and Allied Services* London: HMSO.

Bowles S and Gintis H (1998-9) 'Is Egalitarianism Passé? Homo Reciprocans and the Future of Egalitarian Politics' *The Boston Review* 23, December/January.

Burtless G (1999) 'Squeezed for time? American inequality and the shortage of leisure' *Brookings Review* 17 (4) Fall.

Esping-Andersen G (1990) *The Three Worlds of Welfare Capitalism* Princeton: Princeton University Press

Esping-Andersen G (1999) *Social Foundations of Postindustrial Economies* Oxford, Oxford University Press.

Fraser N (1989) 'Women, Welfare and the Politics of Needs Interpretation' in Fraser *Unruly Practices* Minneapolis: University of Minnesota.

Gutmann A and Thompson D (1996) *Democracy and Disagreement* Cambridge, MA:Harvard University Press

Harrington M (1999) *Care and Equality* New York, Alfred Knopf.

Hobhouse L (1993 [1911]) in Meadowcroft, J (ed) *Liberalism and Other Writings* Cambridge: Cambridge University Press.

Kelly R (1999) 'Nice policy, shame it won't work' *The Guardian* 13 August.

Moller Okin S (1989) *Justice, Gender, and the Family* New York: Basic Books

Quadagno J (1994) *The Color of Welfare* New York, Oxford University Press

Sawhill I (1999) 'From welfare to work: toward a new poverty agenda' *Brookings Review* 17 (4), Fall.

Sevenhuijsen S (1999) 'Caring in the Third Way: The relations between obligation, responsibility and care in Third Way discourse', unpublished mimeo, University of Utrecht

13. An urgent case for modernisation: public policy on women's work

Harriet Harman MP

One of the most striking changes that has taken place over the last 10 years is the increase in mothers of pre-school age children going out to work. This has had an impact in economic as well as social terms. However, the effect has not been properly evaluated and public policy has not yet accommodated the fact that today's children are more likely to have a mother who goes out to work than one who stays at home.

Research by Heather Joshi suggests there is no evidence of harm to children whose mother worked when they were over 12 months and under 5 years old. There is a small benefit to children whose mothers are in employment when they are over one year old, particularly if that work is part-time. However, there is some evidence of a negative effect when the mother works when the child is less than a year old (Joshi et al 2000).

My point is not that all women should go out to work or that they should all stay at home until their child is 12 months old – simply that there is a strong case for giving women with babies and young children a real choice in the matter.

In this chapter I look first at child poverty and the Government's efforts to tackle it. Next, I examine the choices mothers make about going out to work and staying at home, and the way in which public policy has developed over recent decades. I then consider the evidence from research and the implications for public policy. Finally, I argue for a more constructive engagement between social and economic policy and for reform of the machinery of government dealing with work and family.

Three routes to ending child poverty

We know that the effects of poverty in childhood stretch far into adult life. The government have made it a priority to end child poverty and are tackling the financial side of the problem by three main routes. They are using public money to support children, by means of cash benefits and tax credits. They are boosting fathers' income by helping them get into work and making work pay. And they are boosting mothers' income by helping women to improve their skills, and to find work and childcare.

There has been widespread support for the unprecedented increases in Child Benefit and in Income Support for children under 11 in workless households. And although the abolition of the Married Couples Allowance has not been universally popular, the Children's Tax Credit (a tax allowance that goes to families with children, irrespective of marital status) is generally acknowledged as a legitimate way of directing more resources to families with children.

It is also accepted that fathers must be able to provide for their children and that there is a role for government in helping them into work and ensuring that they are better off in work than on benefits. The Government is doing this through the New Deal for the Young Unemployed and the Long-term Unemployed, the Minimum Wage and the Working Families Tax Credit. Reform of the Child Support Agency is designed to ensure that fathers who do not live with their children still continue to support them financially.

However, enhancing the role of mother as breadwinner still causes concern in many quarters. The fact is that without their mothers working, approximately 1.45 million more children would be in poverty. And this is part of what is behind government policies to support mothers in work and to help more mothers into work. The National Childcare Strategy is about reinforcing the drive for improved educational standards by giving children good pre-school education, after school and school holiday clubs. But it is also about helping mothers earn a living. The Working Families Tax Credit supplements low earnings. The majority who will benefit are mothers. New rights to parental and family leave apply to men and women alike. But as women do the lion's share of care in the home it is, in reality, much more likely to be taken by mothers than by fathers. The New Deal for Lone Parents is explicitly designed to help lone mothers off benefit and into work. Though it doesn't force them to work it is firmly based on the view that it is not a good thing for lone mothers to bring up their children on benefit in a household where no-one is ever working.

There is no consensus in government circles, however, about the need to tackle child poverty through helping mothers to be breadwinners. Some are doubtful about it; others are downright opposed. Mothers themselves, always doubting and self-questioning, worry about the effect their absence may be having on their children. And this is not surprising. It is a huge social change, and for most mothers, a new phenomenom. Today, of all mothers who have children under five, 53 per cent (1.6 million) are in employment. Of those, about 1.2 million were themselves brought up by mothers who were not in paid employment. They are bringing up 1.4m children very differently from the way they themselves were brought up. They are redefining motherhood to be about providing for their children as well as caring for them.

What is best for the children

All mothers want what is best for their children. Those who go out to work try to be both good mothers and good breadwinners. There is no doubt that the economy needs their work. Women's work is now vital in all regions and all sectors. If they all left the workforce, the economy would grind to a halt. And as the premium on physical strength reduces and the premium on higher education increases, women's foothold in the labour market is likely to become even firmer. They bring many benefits. Women who have no tradition in the labour market have no set hours to defend, nor any fixed expectations that their work should be done in certain ways and at certain times. They can therefore adapt more easily to changing work patterns. Women who are working to provide for their children are likely to make reliable, long-term employees. They are dependable because their children are depending on them. And as Europe's working-age population shrinks, women's work can help to address the problem of paying for old age. It also protects them, the majority of pensioners, from low income in retirement. No wonder economists tend to be enthusiastic about there being a substantial workforce of well-educated, flexible and reliable women.

There are good reasons why women themselves are enthusiastic about paid work. It is important for the household income and the family standard of living, especially now that there are fewer jobs in the traditional manufacturing industries that can command a 'family wage' (enough to support a dependent spouse and two children). With more marriages breaking down, financial independence starts to look like a sensible personal insurance for women and their children. Fathers' record on child support is so atrocious that most women are obliged to choose between going out to work and subsisting on benefit after a separation. Furthermore, women now leave education with equal qualifications to men's. They can and want to use them to make a contribution to the world outside the home. Improvements in birth control and domestic labour saving devices mean that women now have fewer pregnancies, fewer children and less housework. They have more time, therefore, and more years in the labour market.

For the best part of two decades, women in my Peckham constituency have been saying to me, 'I'm desperate to get back to work...I was good at my work before I had the kids...I'm going mad with the toddler in my flat...he's going mad cooped up in the flat with me all day...I want him to have the same things as other kids.' They want to work, not despite their children but because of them.

Making a commitment

Of course, women's entry into the labour market was well underway long before Labour got into government. The Tories' approach was 'let them get on with it, we are the party of free choice'. But they dared not be seen to encourage this new trend, for fear of accusations that they were undermining the traditional role of mothers in the home. So their policies supported neither the mother at home bringing up children nor the mother combining work and home responsibilities.

By contrast, New Labour has committed itself to supporting the new generation of working women. This is not just as a matter of principle and practicality; it is because the party has needed to win women's votes. Its traditional image had been a problem not only for middle England: the weakness of Labour support among women had been a feature of all elections since 1945. Backing the young working woman made good electoral sense and paid off. At the last election the gender gap almost closed, particularly among young people, which worked in Labour's favour.

So if women are so well entrenched in the world of work what are the doubts surrounding government support? First, there are worries that women's encroachment on the traditional role of men is precipitating a challenge to masculinity – some even call it a crisis. If a man is not the sole provider, nor even the main provider for his family, his role is changed and uncertain. I note this concern, not because I plan to deal with it here but because it is used to support the case against women with young children going out to work. By and large, it is an argument that finds more favour with men and social policy analysts that it does with women.

More troubling are the doubts about how women having jobs outside the home affects their children. This is a huge issue for women: what is the impact on the current generation of children, who have swapped a stay-at-home mother for one who goes out to work? Evidence from abroad that no harm comes to most children from their mother's employment cuts no ice. Neither, apparently, does the reminder that women went out to work during the war when the men were away fighting with no apparent ill effect on that generation of children.

Sifting the evidence

Joshi's research for the Smith Institute sought to shed light on the longer-term outcomes for children who have more of their mother's money but less of their mother's time. I commissioned this work because the Government needed to know the effects of its policies to support women's work, and because women wanted to know whether, generally speaking, the trend towards paid employment, of which they were part, was good or bad for their children.

Existing research by Gregg and Machin, based on the same birth cohort, has already shown the lasting effect of child poverty later in life (Gregg and Machin 1998). Katherine Kiernan has shown how lone mothers can be a strong positive role model for their daughters if they are in paid work by the time they are 16 (Kiernan 1997; Lewis, Kiernan and Land, 1998). The daughters in her study were more likely to do better in education, and in the world of work and were themselves less likely to become teenage mothers than the daughters of lone mothers who did not have jobs.

Joshi's research on Maternal Employment and Child Outcomes looked, for the first time, at the effects of mothers working when their children were very young – under school age. Did the mother's absence have a detrimental effect which thereby undermined, or canceled out altogether, the beneficial effect of the mother's income? Did the fact that the mother was working (irrespective of the income generated) have a beneficial effect on the child?

With the size of the samples in the birth cohort studies we could be confident that any detrimental effect of mother's work would be detected. We found no evidence of this where the mother was working when the child was over a year old. In fact, in these circumstances, the child was slightly less likely to show signs of outward aggression and inward anxiety when it reached school age. Part-time work seemed to be particularly beneficial. That is reassuring news for the government , affirming its strategy of helping children through the mother's income. It is reassuring news for mothers who are going out to work: if their children seem fine, then they probably are. They should trust their instincts.

For the children under a year old there is a barely discernible negative effect – although this is greatly outweighed by the positive effect of the mother working if, by doing so, she protects her children from poverty. We know that most mothers are not keen to rush back to work when their child is still a baby. The Working Families Tax Credit already helps by increasing the family income through topping up the father's pay if the mother's giving up work reduces the family income. But for lone mothers giving up work usually means depending on Income Support and incurring a substantial drop in income. For many mothers in the lowest income families, the break from work after having a baby turns into a long term disconnection from the labour market, in the very families where the mother's income is most important.

We know something about choice and constraints from looking at what happens in firms with different maternity leave policies. Penguin Books, for example, part of the the Pearson Group, gives paid leave for six months and unpaid leave for a further six months. They find that women return after the six months citing the lack of pay as the reason they return, rather than because they feel that they or the baby are ready to do so. This strengthens the case for increasing the mother's choice when her baby is in early infancy.

Policy implications

We should have a package of policies that would increase women's choice about when and how they go back to work. And it should encourage and enable men to play a bigger part in the day to day care of their children. If that happens children will benefit from having more of their father's time, mothers will benefit from being able to share the responsibility of the caring role, and fathers will benefit from being able to form a stronger bond with their children.

Instead, what we currently have is a system that suits neither the mother, nor the father nor the child. It gives the mother maternity pay for 18 weeks only. It puts pressure on her to return to work within six months, where the alternative is to lose her job. It usually means she is required to go back to her job full-time. It will pay a family up to £70 a week for childcare costs when the mother goes back to work but this is not available if the mother stays at home to care for the baby. And it gives fathers the right to time off work, but only unpaid. Furthermore, the current system of

Statutory Maternity Pay and Maternity Allowance is confusing for women and a nightmare for employers to administer.

To give women with babies more choice and to enable fathers to play a greater role, I suggest the following changes:

- Extend the right to return to work up until the baby is 12 months old

- Back extended maternity leave with a new Baby Premium in the Working Families Tax Credit for families with a baby up to 12 months old.

- Give mothers more control over how they work by giving them the right to work part-time after maternity leave, unless the employer can show it would harm the business.

- Pay particular attention to monitoring and promoting the quality of childcare for babies who are under 12 months. This is the area of childcare where there is the greatest unmet demand. It is the most expensive age for childcare but must not be done on the cheap.

- Back parental leave with payment – either universal, flat rate, or only for families eligible for the Working Families Tax Credit.

'Joining up' social and economic policy

There is clearly potential for an interesting debate about the public policy response to any research findings about the effect on children of women working. But the debate is hampered because it crosses over the divide between social and economic policy issues. The old stereotypes require Treasury Ministers and their economists to talk about numbers – the money supply, interest rates, inflation, unemployment levels, growth rates and the relationship between them. Meanwhile Ministers in the so-called 'social policy departments' are expected to discuss people – families, the elderly, children and the relationships between them. And never the twain shall meet. The Treasury should stay out of social policy or stand accused of 'imperialism' and social policy departments should not worry their heads about the economy, it is far too difficult for them and must be left to the Treasury.

But economists have to be concerned about the human capital on whom economic success depends. Home is not just 'where the heart is', but where the human capital is. And social policy analysts have to take account of how the change in our economies and in the world of work affects communities, families and individuals. The technological revolution is changing everything about our economies and the demographic and family revolution is changing just about everything else. To make sensible public policy we need to draw on both disciplines. President Clinton has called for 'putting a human face on economics'. But I think it needs more than that. We need to end the distinction between economic and social policy and move towards a new discipline of 'human economics'. We also need to recognise that the current Government machinery is an obstacle to delivering on these policy issues. Seven Departments of State have an involvement in work and family issues There is no clear departmental lead and for none of them is work and family at the top of the agenda. There are a number of options for changing the machinery of government so that clear leadership and effective delivery can be brought to bear upon these issues.

These include, first, to create a new agency for work and family (analogous to the Food Standards Agency, which bridges the gap between the Ministry of Agriculture, Fisheries and Food, and the Department of Health). The second option would be to establish a unit in the Cabinet Office with a lead minister whose sole responsibility is children. The third would be to create a new department of Work and Family, which would draw together all the issues of social and economic policy for those of working age. This would take all benefits for those of working age and the employment functions that are currently spread between the Department for Education and Employment and the Department of Trade and Industry. It would probably mean that the Department of Social Security would become too small to remain as a separate department and would need to be re-merged with the Department of Health.

Governments are always keen just to 'get on with it' and dread the turf wars and distractions that inevitably beset the task of trying to change departmental boundaries. Ministers in post have a vested interest in keeping and building their empires, rather than proposing reforms that might lead to boundary changes. But the current system reflects an out-dated society in which work and home were separate spheres. That is manifestly no longer the case. We therefore need a vigorous debate on how policies can be brought into line with life as it is really lived today, and then a determination radically to reform the machinery of government to deliver it.

References

Gregg P and Machin S (1998) *Child Development and Success or Failure in the Youth Labour Market* London: London School of Economics, Centre for Economic Performance, Discussion paper 397.

Joshi H, Verropulou G, Harman H and Stevenson W (2000) *Maternal Employment and Child Outcomes: analysis of two birth cohort studies* London: Smith Institute.

Kiernan K (1997) *The Legacy of Parental Divorce: Social, economic and demographic experiences in adulthood* London: London School of Economics, Centre for Analysis of Social Exclusion, Paper 1.

Lewis J, Kiernan K and Land H (1998) *Lone Motherhood in Twentieth-century Britain: from footnote to front page* Oxford: Oxford University Press.

13. Better work for all
Matthew Taylor and Alexandra Jones

Campaigning for radical improvement in the quality of paid employment should now be a priority for the centre left. And if the campaign is to succeed it must draw on the experience and insights feminists have developed over decades of struggle for equality in the workplace. In this chapter we outline the scale of poor quality employment and then describe the main elements in the feminist struggle for better terms and conditions for women. We argue that the campaign for better work must be one that engages all types of workers, women and men, parents and non-parents, young and old, well-paid and low-paid. Finally, we suggest that the struggle for better work must be linked to a wider critique of the values of consumer capitalism.

Better work: a second term issue

For those in work, employment is a central element of identity. But work also defines everyone else; children are asked what they want to be when they grow up, older citizens are described in terms of their former professions. And those who are unable to get work are more likely to suffer poverty, ill health and depression.

Our life chances and those of our children, our social status, our health – all of these are in large part shaped by our success or lack of it in the labour market. And everyone from philosophers to psychotherapists tells us our experience of work is central to our sense of well-being and personal fulfilment.

Not until the onset of the Industrial Revolution did employment become widely and closely associated with personal status and identity. That was the time at which 'work' became associated with a 'job' performed outside the home, often in severely hazardous circumstances, in mills, mines and factories. Since then workplace conditions have been steadily improved through governmental regulation, trade union brokered collective agreements and technological change. Now, in the context of virtually full employment (at least in some parts of the UK), there is room for further advances in the quality of employment.

Of course quality of work means different things to different people. To some, pay is all-important, to others, hours are more significant. There are others who would measure the quality of employment by the level of their autonomy in work, by the quality of their friendships with workmates and colleagues, or by the contribution they felt they were making to society at large. Behind these diverse viewpoints lie three crucial questions: do we enjoy our work, is it worthwhile, are we successful at it? Those who can answer 'yes' to all are happy indeed, but they are in a minority. As Suzanne Franks has argued, in a global marketplace, where the 'job for life' is a thing of the past, it is 'the individual rather than the company [that] has to adapt to the changing patterns and demands of the labour market and to absorb the insecurities that were previously contained within institutions'(Franks 1999). Millions work longer hours than they want, have jobs that are mundane and lack scope for training and personal development, and find it difficult to balance work with the other things they want to do in their lives.

Work that does not offer job satisfaction, training and career development, flexibility and a balance with other responsibilities and needs is bad for productivity and bad for the economy. Poor quality work undermines our capacity to be good parents and good citizens. Work that devalues caring and traditionally female roles, through poor pay and poor social recognition, is bad for society. And inequalities in the world of work mirror and reinforce other forms of inequality.

How important is the reform of work for Labour's second term in office? The facts speak for themselves:

- According to the European Commission (1995) Britain has the longest working hours in Europe, and average weekly hours have increased over the last decade:
    - In 1998, 84 per cent of male employees and 45 per cent of female employees were usually working more than 40 hours a week (compared with 73 per cent and 27 per cent respectively for 1988)
    - 30 per cent of men and 10 per cent of women were working more than 50 hours a week in 1998 (comparative figures for 1988 were 24 per cent and four per cent respectively)(Labour Force Survey 1998, Spring Figures).

- In a quarter of two parent households at least one parent works regularly in the evenings (Harkness 1999)

- On average, training contributes towards an employee gaining higher wages and transferable skills. However, it remains unequally distributed, with the least training going to those with the least formal education and the lower status jobs (Green 1999)

- Approximately 40 per cent of employees are dissatisfied with their job (Mori 1999)

- 41 per cent of employees believe that work pressures affect their personal life (Mori 1999)

The need for better work is manifest. But the momentum for change lies not only in an altruistic desire to improve the lives of citizens. Many parts of the South East of England are experiencing full employment. In times of high national unemployment, governments tend to view the quality of work as a second-order issue. But the shift towards a sellers' labour market in parts of the country should make it more important for employers to demonstrate that their work is good work and this, in turn, will empower employees to be more demanding about their conditions. The Government will find itself needing to manage rising aspirations and expectations amongst workers and their representatives.

Any consideration of the future shape of work must address the impact of technological change. New technologies seem to offer opportunities for more flexible working in which employees have access to more information, and more complex and engaging work, and are able to work from wherever they choose. But for everyone willing to predict a better future (McRae H 1998) there are others who point to deteriorating working conditions - suggesting, for example, that call centres could be 'the factory sweatshops of the future' (Fernie & Metcalf 1998). There is a danger of technology driving a process of polarisation in which semi-skilled jobs are replaced with more managerial and supervisory roles, but also with more mundane service sector jobs. Technology has the potential both to empower and to enslave.

'Better work' will be an increasingly insistent issue for both employers and politicians. Change will require commitment not only from business but also from public policy makers, along with pressure from voters and key interest groups such as trade unions. Improving the quality of work should thus be a key aim of the centre left. In pursuing this aim there is much to be learnt from the feminist struggle for equality at work.

Feminism and the pursuit of equality in the workplace

Employment has long been central to feminist thought and campaigning. Broadly, four strands can be identified.

One has been the demand for formal equality in the workplace, realised through such measures as the Equal Pay and Sex Discrimination Acts, implemented in 1975, and a series of Directives from the European Union.

The second has challenged the informal barriers to women's advancement. Twenty-four years after the equalities legislation came into force, only 32 per cent of managers and administrators are women. Women also remain concentrated within certain areas of employment, with 83 per cent of women working in the service industries compared with 56 per cent of men (EOC 1999). The 'glass ceiling' became a focus of feminist campaigning in the 1980s. The issue was taken up by (among others) the Conservative government, who sponsored 'Opportunity 2000'to encourage employers to promote women, and by the 300 Group and Emily's List, all-party organisations established to promote the selection and election of women as MPs. The campaign for a minimum wage can also be seen as part of this strand, addressing the persistent association of women's work with low pay.[1]

The third strand recognises that women – especially mothers - tend to have different needs from men, and calls for special measures to accommodate them. This has had some resonance with New Labour in government. Key initiatives include the New Deal for Lone Parents, expansion of pre-school provision under the national child-care strategy and the introduction of child care tax credits. Although most of these initiatives are targeted at parents, in reality it is overwhelmingly mothers who are the main beneficiaries. Increasingly feminist debates are focusing upon this issue, and are arguing for the need to share childcare responsibilities more equally between women and men.

The fourth element is closely related to the third and centres on the call for family friendly employment. Concretely, the focus is on the provision of leave and flexible working, and on childcare provision for both parents. The introduction of the Working Time Regulations in October 1998, with their provision for paid holidays and the legal right to limit hours of work, and the Employment Relations Act, which implemented the Parental Leave Directive in December 1999 and provided for parental leave and emergency family leave, were important steps. The demand – made primarily on grounds of social equity - for parental leave to be paid is figuring highly in debates about New Labour's priorities for the remainder of its first term and for its manifesto for re-election. Evidence that a third of working mothers are quitting full time jobs for part time positions or giving up work entirely is fuelling demands for a statutory right for parents to return to work on a part-time basis (Avon 2000).[2]

These demands – for the removal of formal and informal barriers to equal treatment and for special measures to accommodate the needs of working parents - continue to be relevant to the implementation of 'better work'. However, these debates must form part of a broader critique of modern work, one that is relevant to all types of workers.

Good work – broadening the alliance

To achieve a successful alliance between business, public policy makers, voters and interest groups, 'better work' campaigners must first address the public perception that their proposed reforms are only relevant to a limited section of the population. Engagement usually requires a degree of self-interest. What has been called family friendly policy is now being re-branded as 'work-life balance' in an attempt to shift the focus away from parents (particularly mothers) towards all employees, emphasising the relevance of 'better work' to broader sections of society. Three issues in particular need to be addressed in order for this re-branding to be successful and for broader support to be engaged for the campaign.

First, family-friendly polices should be reformed to ensure that they are available to all families: fathers as well as mothers, low-paid workers as well as those on higher incomes. Suppositions about income levels and about who has domestic responsibilities, that are implicit in current policies, must be challenged. Feminist writers have highlighted the invisible nature of unpaid domestic labour, the majority of which falls upon the shoulders of women, even if they are employed.[3] Slowly, men are beginning to be more active in the domestic sphere and as fathers (Burghes, et al 1997). If this is to continue, and a more equal division of responsibility in the home is to be achieved, the assumption that women should bear the brunt of domestic labour must be formally repudiated. Family-friendly policies must ensure that the role of fathers can be recognised and their potential realised by providing 'better work' for them through leave and other forms of flexible working.

Policy must also recognise the realities of an unequal labour market. As Lisa Harker argues (1999) 'family friendly policies have, by and large, been developed with a particular type of worker in mind: a woman, normally a second earner, but certainly with sufficient household income to sustain some fluctuations in earnings'. The point was underlined when a Labour Government committed to social justice introduced new rights to parental leave, but made no provision for payment. These rights are likely to increase existing inequalities in the capacity of different social classes to balance work and home. Put simply, poor parents will not be able to afford to take advantage of the leave on offer. And, where men still tend to be the main breadwinner in two-earner families, they are even less likely to take up the opportunity. For families to become engaged in the campaign, 'better work' must offer both mothers and fathers, regardless of income levels, the opportunity to balance their work with their domestic responsibilities.

Second, while it is important to make flexible working and parental leave accessible to both mothers and fathers, reform of employment cannot assume that all workers either are or will be parents. Some workers have no caring responsibilities; others are not parents but care for elderly or disabled dependants. The importance of flexibility being available to all employees should be emphasised.

Some of the difficult questions that must be addressed if the campaign for better work is to be inclusive and effective were raised in an episode of the popular and post-feminist drama Ally McBeal. The story line involved a senior law firm partner – a caricature career woman with no life outside work - representing a male employer accused of sex discrimination. The employer stands accused of failing to promote a female worker because she insists on balancing career and family by working regulation hours. In defending the employer, the lawyer asks the court to consider her own experience. Why, she asks, should a woman who has chosen to deny herself the joys of motherhood and family life in pursuit of success at work find her extra dedication to her job overlooked when being compared with a mother? After all, as she argues, no other employee (including a father) would expect advancement without being willing to work the very long hours expected of well-paid career professionals.

To avoid a reaction, of which there is already some evidence in the United States,[4] against the implication that only mothers are entitled to balanced work, reformers must ensure that the call for family friendly working be seen as only the first step in a campaign for work-life balance. In this way the campaign can be joined not just by women but by men, not just by parents but by the increasing number of those who want to combine work with caring for dependants such as elderly relatives, by those who want to volunteer in the community, and by older people able and willing to work well into their seventies.

Moving towards an ultimate goal of 'work-life' balance also requires that younger employees be targeted. Inflexible work hours can only be tackled if both younger and more experienced workers can actively see advantages in flexibility. Time banks, in which employees invest hours of work, could strike a particular chord with this generation. The opportunity to invest long hours worked whilst an employee has no responsibility for a dependant could be used to accrue reduced hours when these are required. Thus employees would be able to use their 'invested time' to take on domestic responsibilities, or perhaps pursue qualifications or other interests. This could both ensure that moving in and out of work and caring is less problematic, as well as engaging a crucial section of the population for whom families and caring might seem a distant prospect. Time spent on qualifications also improves prospects for career development and access to higher quality work, which would be of particular benefit to those with lower educational attainments early on in life.

Third, a successful campaign cannot just focus on the issue of flexibility, but must also address the qualitative inequalities within the labour market. Low pay, low skills, low opportunities and low status cluster together in the labour market.

Feminist experience in campaigning for equality in real, rather than merely formal, terms can again contribute to broadening the agenda beyond flexibility. Women make up 76 per cent of the lowest income group (EOC 1999), and it is those individuals who are on the lowest wages who suffer the most from poor quality work. Despite research showing that jobs that satisfy employees and give them a sense of autonomy tend to be more productive (West & Patterson 1999), the case for enlightened self-interest on the part of employers, made by bodies such as the Industrial Society and the Institute of Personnel and Development, has failed to convince the majority. Individuals employed in the service sector, and at the lower end of the labour market, are gaining little or no advantage from family friendly or work/life policies. Lower paid workers are less likely to receive training, less likely to have any control over the work process, more likely to suffer accidents at work, more likely to work unsociable hours, and less likely to have managers who will show flexibility in the face of demands outside work.

The defence of wide and widening inequalities in working life, tends to be made in terms that are either functional 'someone has got to do the menial work' or elitist 'lots of people only want to do routine work'. These arguments are reminiscent of the case against equal pay made on the ground that women worked for 'pin money'. This elitist view should be questioned. Even if some people do want routine work, this does not mean their jobs must be tedious or stressful or that they should be left without any voice or control. As research into call centre management has found, even apparently routine work can be managed in ways that provide greater job satisfaction, job flexibility and opportunities for training and career development. Fernie and Holman (2000) argue that management policies are more successful when they reflect the human aspects of the work, rather than simply utilising the monitoring technology available. Their findings suggest that giving employees greater control over their work, providing adequate training and coaching, and having a supportive management structure has an enormous impact upon well-being and job satisfaction within these alleged 'sweatshops'.

More fundamentally, we should question the view that there are millions of people with only very limited lifetime aspirations for the shape and content of their work. Are these limited aspirations really limited expectations? Until quite recently it was widely accepted by policy makers that the poor educational achievement of the majority was functional for a society where most jobs were unskilled. But if the Government is aiming to raise everyone's expectations of their educational potential, isn't it equally legitimate and necessary to raise expectations of their potential at work?

While Labour is highly interventionist – even authoritarian – in insisting that the public sector raise expectations and achievements in schools and colleges, the Government relies on little more than exhortation to improve the quality of employment and training in the economy as a whole. Sights should be set higher for a second term.

Choosing better work

The reform of work is part of the pursuit of social justice. But it also poses new political challenges and raises fundamental questions about our relationship to work, both as a society and individually.

Primarily, questions arise about our understanding of what constitutes 'proper work'. Our differing perceptions of paid employment and unpaid domestic labour have a crucial impact upon our conception of the type of work that should be valued. Feminists have attempted to measure the scale of unpaid labour and its impact on individual families and society (see Folbre 1993). They have argued that the domestic (predominantly female) sphere is rendered invisible within economic theory, which is principally concerned with the occupational (traditionally male) sphere (Cox 1993). They have questioned the assumption by champions of both capital and labour (and, on the strength of current policies, New Labour) that 'real' work is work in the formal economy and that social progress should be exclusively measured by growth in that economy and the distribution of its wealth (see Rich, 1976 and Gibson-Graham, 1996).

Natasha Walters has argued that the constructed division between the public and private sphere inhibits the reform of work. She challenges 'ordinary women and men to raise their voices and demand the revolution in working life they desire'. Advocating a transformation of work so that the 'linear' way of living associated with paid employment can be reconciled with the 'cyclical' nature of domestic life, Walter asserts that 'if the wall that has been set up between work and home could be knocked down, we could move to a more equal society' (Walter, 1998).

Walter is optimistic about the possibilities for more flexible work, quoting the potential of technology and the thinking of such management gurus as Charles Handy. But before we can choose better work we may have to change more than just our perceptions of the occupational and domestic spheres. A broad alliance for better work requires acknowledgement that 'better' is a subjective view.

This brings us back to Ally McBeal's career-centred colleague. Part of her argument is that, faced with the dichotomy between work and home, different people must be free to make different choices. This must be confronted if the protagonists of better work are not to appear unrealistic or paternalistic. Although many employees work longer hours and under more pressure than they would choose, many others prefer to work longer and harder than absolutely necessary. The motives involved may be instrumental (career or income enhancement); they may be driven by enjoyment of work (job satisfaction, commitment to the team or organisation), or they may be influenced by the limitations of life outside work (for many people, work can be the main or only source of sociability). In truth, many people find life at work more congenial than life outside. When confronted by calls for his resignation, former Conservative Minister Nicolas Ridley is said to have retorted 'I have no desire to spend more time with my family'.

There are two issues here, both of which have strong echoes in feminist discourse. First, while challenging the status quo, we must be wary of appearing to argue there is one optimal way for people to live their lives. Despite what feminists actually argued (and of course there are diverse forms of feminism) it has been possible to caricature the pursuit of equality at work and better childcare as a drive by women to put progress in paid employment above other forms of fulfilment. This led authors such as Adrienne Rich to call for the re-evaluation of typically female characteristics. She argued that analysing society from a female stance, rather than automatically adopting the work-oriented values of a male-dominated world, would demonstrate the importance of typically female caring and maternal roles.

Despite these counter-arguments, the perception that feminists deprecated unpaid caring remained. They became scapegoats for a range of social problems – 'latch key children', for example - which periodically become the focus of a moral panic around the effects of maternal employment on children. The aims of work flexibility must be clear. This is not about abandoning parental responsibilities; nor is it about any form of 'social engineering' or 'nanny statism' (to which charges the left is always vulnerable). The aim must be (and must be seen to be) not to prescribe one course of action, but to increase choice. However, in doing so we must be clear about the social and economic construction of choice.

While most would acknowledge an aspiration to have a better work-life balance, the difficulty is deciding whether it should be the state, the individual or the employer who bears the costs of this choice. The debate over this will continue, but it is the individual who must ultimately reconcile the necessary trade-off between money and time, and this reconciliation is not an easy one. On the one hand, choices are constrained by economic realities, especially for the poor. In a society with huge disparities in income and wealth, the pressure will remain to work long and hard and on whatever terms are offered . On the other hand most people do not simply work to earn enough to meet basic human needs. Work gives us social status and enables us to participate in the consumer culture. To the full time mother who dreads the casual question 'and what do you do?' add the low-income parent explaining to their children that it doesn't matter if they don't have Nike trainers.

Second, to Walters' rejection of narrow ideas of productive labour we must add a critique of the consumer culture that tells us 'we are what we spend'. Susan Faludi in her major study of American men (1999) argues that men are now suffering the effects of the alienating consumer culture that first gave rise to modern feminism. She reminds us that many of the key early works of this movement – including Betty Friedan's *The Feminine Mystique* – were broadsides not at men per se but at the 'commercial mistreatment of women'. Faludi quotes from Sheila Ballentyne's *Norma Jean the Termite Queen*:

> 'What's the matter with you, Norma' the husband Martin asks when he returns one evening to find his Pleasant Valley housewife half catatonic, staring at an ad for household appliances 'Do you want a new microwave oven? Do you want a new kitchen floor? How about redecorating the bathroom?' 'No', she replies 'I want to die, Martin'.

Faludi concludes

> The commercialised, ornamental 'femininity' that the women's movement diagnosed now has men by the throat. Men and women both feel cheated of lives in which they might have contributed to a social world; men and women feel pushed into roles that are about little more than displaying

prettiness or prowess in the market place. Women were pushed first, but now their brothers have joined the same forced march. (Faludi 1999, p602)

Of course, people can and do choose to live a balanced life. Not everyone chooses the job with the highest income. Not everyone feels compelled to conform to commodified notions of beauty and status. Parents do try to imbue their children with values other than consumerism. But those on the left should recognise the insights of thinkers such as Walter and Faludi – that radical change must involve articulating values different from those of consumer capitalism. In short, the argument for better work must also be an argument for a society where being a good father is as important as being a high achiever, where being a good citizen is more highly valued than being an ostentatious consumer.

Conclusion

New Labour's first term has been characterised by a policy framework in which the maximisation of employment has been the central device for addressing social inequality. Nearing the end of this term, job creation and economic management are amongst the major achievements of the Blair Government. Calling for quality of work as well as quantity does not imply a departure from existing policy. There is no incompatibility between the statements 'any job is better than no job' and 'a good job is better than a bad job'.

We do not need a revolution to have better jobs. Good work is compatible with profitability and economic growth. But to make the strongest case for change we need to think big; to ask how we want to live our lives and structure our society. We need to question whether the market on its own will deliver the forms of employment that fit our needs. We need to argue for greater equality in access to flexible work, training and other measures of job satisfaction. As a first step, we need to recognise the particular needs of groups such as parents and carers, and acknowledge state responsibilities to the dependants they care for. But we also need to argue that society as a whole should have more control over the way that it works.

Thus far, assailed by the day-to-day demands of office, New Labour has shown little enthusiasm for radical questions about work. Its emphasis has been on quantitative measures of economic progress. Its aim has been to include the excluded. This suggests that, if New Labour were to develop an agenda of employment reform, it could be too narrow in its focus, too modest in its goals – and therefore only relevant to a minority. 'Work-life' should refer to a balance between a rewarding job with scope for individual development and involvement in activities outside paid work.

The case for better work should be broad and deep, every step forward must be valued, but progress must be driven by a vision of a society in which work serves us rather then the reverse. Over many decades women in general and feminists in particular have developed experience of campaigning for changes to the organisation of employment, have challenged the economistic assumptions of the male dominated labour and trade union movement, and have articulated radically different values and visions. This experience and insight can now drive the next leap forward at work.

Thanks to Lisa Harker and Nick Burkitt for comments on an earlier draft of this chapter.

Endnotes

1   Recent research conducted for the Women's Unit found that being a woman directly affects pay levels. It found that a mid-skilled childless woman is estimated to earn £241,000 less than their male counterpart over their lifetime, whilst for women with children, there is a further gap ('a mother gap') of £140,000.

2   Comparisons of parental leave policies within Europe demonstrate the success of these rights in countries such as Sweden and the Netherlands.

3   This has been a constant refrain since the 1960s, see: Friedan, B (1963) *The Feminine Mystique* London: Gollancz; Pateman, C (1988) *The Sexual Contract* Cambridge: Polity Press; Greer, G (1999) *The Whole Woman* New York: AA Knopf: 119-123

4   Elinor Burkett, who has written extensively upon the situation of contemporary women within the US, has recently published 'The Baby Boon: How Family-Friendly America Cheats the Childless' (March 2000).

References

Avon Longitudinal Study of Pregnancy and Children University of Bristol, 2000.

Burghes L, Clarke L & Cronin N (1997) *Fathers and Fatherhood in Britain* Family Policies Study Centre

Cox E (1993) 'The Economics of Mutual Support: A feminist approach' in Rees, S *et al Beyond the Market* Leichhardt, NWS: Pluto Press

EOC (1999)

European Commission Figures 1995.

Fernie S & Holman D (2000) 'Can I Help You?: Call centres and job satisfaction' in *Centrepiece* Centre for Economic Performance, London School of Economics (Feb 2000)

Fernie S & Metcalf D (1998) 'Hanging on the Telephone' in *Centrepiece* Centre for Economic Performance, London School of Economics (Feb 1998, issue 11)

Folbre, N (1993) *Who Pays for the Kids? Gender and the structures of constraint* New York & London: Routledge

Franks S (1999) *Having none of it: women, men and the future of work* London: Granta Books

Gibson-Graham J K (1996) *The end of capitalism (as we knew it): A Feminist critique of Political Economy* Oxford: Blackwell

Green F (1999), 'Training the Workers' Gregg P & Wadsworth J (eds) *The State of Working Britain* Manchester: Manchester University Press

Harker L (1999) *Family-friendly policies in a modern labour market* unpublished working paper IPPR

Harkness S (1999) 'Working 9 to 5' in Gregg P & Wadsworth J (eds) *The State of Working Britain* Manchester: Manchester University Press

MORI (1999)

McRae H 'Jobs will soon be flexible, fulfilling and fun' *The Guardian* (25.03.98)

West & Patterson (1999) 'The workforce and productivity: People management is the key to c losing the productivity gap' in *New Economy* Vol 6, issue 1

Rich A (1976) *Of Woman Born: Motherhood as Experience and Institution* New York: Norton

Walter N (1998) *The New Feminism* London: Little, Borwn & Co

Faludi S (1999) *Stiffed: the betrayal of the American man* New York: W Morrow & Co

14. Equal partners in the family? Views, preferences and policy dilemmas

Ruth Kelly

Family policy has often been trapped in a sterile debate between those who see women's role as in the home, and those who argue that women should be competing equally in the workforce with men and contributing equally to the family income. Neither model of the family accurately reflects the social reality – full-time, dual-earner couples with young children are still relatively rare – nor does either model reflect what women themselves consider their role to be today. Above all, women are the ones to recognise that the new opportunities on offer in the labour market are difficult to embrace without a drastic change in the relations between men, women and children. The decline of the 'family' wage has meant that women's contribution to the household income has become increasingly important. But without men embracing parental and domestic responsibilities, women will always tend to find themselves in low-wage, low-skill, part-time jobs, without the opportunities available to men. Nor do women – who still consider themselves to be primarily responsible for the family – wish to relinquish the choice to stay at home with children, particularly those below school age, in the fight for equal status in the labour market. This changing social reality opens up acute dilemmas for policy-makers. Should the state prefer one model of family life over another? Or be neutral between family choices? The following chapter attempts to tease out some of the implications for policy of different views and preferences regarding the family.

Changing patterns of work

The increasing participation of women in the labour force has been well-documented: 62 per cent of couples with dependent children are now in work. The biggest increase in participation is among women with young children. Over half of married and cohabiting women with pre-school children are working today, compared with 45 per cent in 1988, reflecting the fact that women are returning sooner and not leaving employment during maternity leave. Nearly 12 per cent of women with pre-school age children work more than 40 hours a week (Labour Market Trends, 1999).

This has meant that women are making a greater-than-ever contribution to the family budget, and their labour is often vital to the household finances. In 1977-81, only one in 15 women contributed more to the family budget than their partner, but by 1989-91, one in five did so. Women earned on average around a quarter of family income in 1979-81. Nowadays they earn around one third of family income, with full-time women workers earning around 40 per cent of family income (Harkness, 1995).

There is little evidence that the increase of women in paid employment has been matched by a commensurate change in the way domestic tasks are divided within households, however. Women are now expected to contribute to the family income – but are also expected to place family and domestic needs first. Even when women are in full-time employment they appear to remain primarily responsible for both childcare and domestic chores. The latest British Social Attitudes Survey asked those living with a partner or spouse which of them did a variety of different household chores. Respondents could say that a chore was usually or always done by a woman, by a man, or by both, or that it was done by another person altogether. Seventy-nine per cent of couples reported that women always or usually did the washing and ironing in the house – and when this was narrowed down to British households where the woman earned the same or more than her partner, this figure dropped only to 63 per cent.

Contradictions regarding the importance of family and work, as well as the tensions that surround modern gender roles, are putting a new strain on the relationships at the centre of family life. As Ulrich Beck, in his consideration of the contradicting demands posed by marriage and the labour market, points out:

> The contradiction…could only remain hidden so long as it was taken for granted that marriage meant renunciation of a career for women, responsibility for children and 'comobility' according to the professional destiny of the husband. The contradiction bursts open when both spouses must or want to be free to earn a living as a salary earner (Beck, 1992).

The policy response

Many governments have chosen to respond to the decline of the traditional male breadwinner model by promoting an alternative which has been described by Jane Lewis, Professor of Social Policy at Oxford University, as an 'Adult-Citizen-Worker' model. This is a model in which state cash allowances are given to families to buy in domestic and childcare services, while employment is promoted equally for men and women (both those in couples and lone parents). It attempts to compensate women for the costs of taking time out from the labour market around the birth of a child. The short-run costs of time-off, such as loss of income, and the long-term costs, such as loss of career opportunities and pension entitlements, are explicitly recognised and to some extent compensated for – by maternity pay, anti-sex discrimination laws in the workplace and credits to pension schemes for those caring for very young children. Many argue that, without full participation in the labour force, women are leaving themselves financially vulnerable to the possibility of abandonment by their partner, or indeed, poverty in old age.

In Britain, family policy under New Labour has so far concentrated on making work pay for low-income families, and enabling them to have access to good quality, affordable childcare. The working families' tax credit (WFTC) tops up the income of low-income households with children, the minimum wage sets a floor under earnings, and the childcare tax credit will subsidise childcare places for the first two children on a sliding scale in low to middle-income families. The new stakeholder pension will credit women caring for young children as if they were in work (albeit low-paid work). The National Childcare Strategy is an unprecedented £8 billion programme to overcome obstacles that women face when returning to work.

The proposals to make work pay have gone hand in hand with a strategy to encourage lone parents back into work – with the primary motivation of decreasing dependency and creating a working role model for children in such households, widening the horizons of the next generation.

Even if you accept that social norms are changing, it would be more realistic to argue, however, that any viable model of the family in which women's labour force participation is central should recognise both mother and father explicitly as parents – a 'Parent-Citizen-Worker' model or, perhaps, if other forms of caring are also explicitly recognised, a 'Carer-Citizen-Worker' model. Responsible fatherhood is critical to women's opportunities in the labour market. Without a supportive, responsible husband and father, women and children tend to live in poverty, and it is exceptionally difficult for women to have enough domestic and caring support in the home to be fully involved in the workplace.

That means gearing employment policy towards the needs of men as fathers as well as women as mothers – promoting horizontal gender equity as a core policy objective. This model sees family-friendly policies in the workplace as the way to promote equal parenting. Initiatives such as paid parental leave and a strategy to 'mainstream' fatherhood take on highly symbolic as well as practical value. This is the policy framework in Sweden, which as a result has seen a huge increase in full-time women's labour market participation in recent years, and in Denmark where it is not now unusual for both father and mother to take part-time employment in the first few years after having a child.

The design of individual family-friendly initiatives also becomes crucial to the impact of the policy on gender equity. For example, take parental leave, a flagship policy for the Government's family-friendly employment agenda. As other contributors have pointed out, parental leave as it stands, unpaid, is likely to be used largely by women, who are more willing to sacrifice the time and pay from their jobs not least because they are still likely to be lower-paid than those of their partners. The Government has estimated that while 35 per cent of women are likely to use their parental leave entitlement, only two per cent of men will do so. International experience also suggests that men are highly unlikely to take leave unless it is generously paid. The likely result of unpaid parental leave is therefore that gender inequities are exacerbated in the workplace, rather than narrowed. By contrast, parental leave paid at a high earnings-replacement ratio is much more likely to be taken up by men as well as women, enabling a fairer division of labour in the household and more equal parenting between partners. In Norway, for example, the introduction of a 'daddy quota' of parental leave paid for four weeks, with the payment reserved for fathers, led to a massive reversal in behaviour. Fewer than five per cent of men took leave before the policy change, compared with 80 per cent after the payment was introduced (Leira, 1998).

Other policies such as integrating parenting classes with the New Deal for young fathers, and encouraging all Government services – such as Social Services, midwifery and health visiting – to recognise the needs of fathers as well as mothers, could contribute to making committed fatherhood more socially acceptable. Employers also need to be made more responsive to the needs of the male workforces. There have been successful experiments in the US, sending taskforces into large companies to meet employers and talk to their workforces about the importance of fatherhood, which could be adapted for the UK.

What women want

The problem with the Parent/Carer- Citizen-Worker model is that it does not reflect current preferences in the majority of families. While it is clear that most families have moved away from the traditional male breadwinner – stay-at-home mother model, it is not clear how many have embraced the concepts of shared parenting and dual careers.

The chart below shows that attitudes in Britain are considerably more supportive of full-time working mothers than in countries such as Germany and Ireland, but there is still a strong social consensus in favour of women staying at home when children are below school age, with almost six in ten people questioned saying that a pre-school child is likely to suffer if his or her mother works.

Views on combining work and family life, 1994

	West Germany	Britain	Irish Republic	Nether-lands	Sweden
A working mother can establish just as warm and secure a relationship with her children as a mother who does not work (% agree)	72	63	61	70	64
A pre-school child is likely to suffer if his/her mother works (% disagree)	17	42	41	34	46
All in all, family life suffers when the woman has a full-time job (% disagree)	23	50	38	36	45

Source: British – and European – Social Attitudes Survey 1999

The 'Listening to Women' consultation carried out by the Government in 1999 made some very clear points. It underlined the fact that, in general, women consider themselves primarily, as mothers, responsible for the family – and that their experience as mothers has a major, if not the main, impact on their income and employment patterns. And while many choose to take up the career or job opportunities afforded to them, others deliberately choose not to and are prepared to sacrifice substantial income and career opportunities to stay at home – at least for a period. In particular, the consultation showed that women still consider family-friendly employment as largely their domain: women who choose to work want supportive and flexible arrangements to enable them to balance work and home; but those who choose to stay at home want their role as a wife and mother to be valued and respected.

This desire to have more flexibility in the workplace, and to spend more time at home with young children, is illustrated in recent surveys by the Daycare Trust which show that 87 per cent of mothers of pre-school age children would prefer to stay at home and look after their own children, if money were not a problem. In addition, 31 per cent of mothers working full-time would prefer to work fewer hours with the childcare arrangement of their choice.

There are few signs, futhermore, that the Parent-Citizen-Worker model will start to dominate all other choices in the future. Catherine Hakim has argued in a recent paper, for example, that three quite different, even conflicting, models of the family, and of women's roles, continue to attract roughly equal support across the EU as a whole and within individual EU countries – as well as across educational groups (Hakim, 1999). She names three categories: 'home-centred' women (10-30 per cent), who prefer not to work and give priority to children and family throughout their life; 'work-centred' women, whose main priority is not motherhood (10-30 per cent); and 'adaptive' women (40-80 per cent) who want to combine employment and family without either taking over and are sensitive to the prevailing policy environment.

In Sweden, which offers strong financial inducements to work and good quality early years childcare, for example, mothers with children (under seven) still work on average only 19.1 hours outside the home, compared with 44.8 hours for the average father (SCB, 1990-1). This suggests that although some couples will choose to have dual careers, it is likely that preferences will always remain diverse, with a significant number – if not most – couples choosing for the mother to care for children while they are young and work part-time or not at all.

It is clear that what women really want is choice: the ability to choose to be a responsible parent, nurturing and providing for children, and the ability to find fulfilling employment in or out of the home. The fact is that certainly today – and possibly indefinitely – most mothers would choose to stay at home with young children, if the choice were financially neutral, and return to work part-time once their children reached school age; only later in life, would most women consider returning to work full-time. If such choices are to be excercised without undue constraints, women need employment opportunities, flexibility at work, good quality affordable childcare and the financial option to stay at home.

Policies to encourage the caring role of mothers have been pursued in some European countries, particularly in Germany – which is resistant to the idea of the Adult-Citizen-Worker model – and both Norway and Finland, which emphasise choice. In 1998, Norway, for example, introduced a 'home-care benefit' for families who, through choice or necessity, do not use a state-funded childcare place. Finland also introduced a similar scheme in which a parent can choose to stay at home to look after children in the first three years of the child's life, while being specifically funded by the state; the result has been a massive uptake by around 70 per cent of eligible families – with the women being the main choice of carer. In Britain, the Government has centred its rhetoric of choice around the substantial increase in child benefit since Labour came to power and is now proposing an Integrated Child Credit, which has the potential at least to lower the 'family penalty' for parents who choose to care for their children at home. But it is clear that, if choice is to be a reality, and women's caring role to be properly valued by society, the caring role needs to be explicitly recognised and policy geared to that end.

The options

How government values each model of family life will be implicit in the types of family policy pursued over the coming years. The chart below lists some of the policies the Government might wish to pursue, according to which model of the family it favours and some illustrative costings to the Exchequer of enacting such policies.

Parent-Citizen-Worker Model	
Policies	Cost
Paid parental leave at a high replacement ratio[1]	£2 billion
Paid paternity leave[2]	£360 million
Fatherhood strategy to mainstream fatherhood – including incorporating parenting into the New Deal	na
Flexible working for men and women	na
Enhanced maternity pay for first 18 weeks[3]	£560 million

1 13 weeks per parent paid at full replacement value. Take-up assumptions based on answers to the question 'How many weeks parental leave would you take if money were not a problem' taken from ICM poll (April 2000) on parental leave and costed by KPMG.

2 Costings of paternity leave paid for ten days at 90% earnings replacement value from answer to Parliamentary Question, supplied to Ruth Kelly

3 Based on 90 per cent earnings replacement for 18 weeks; costings from HoC Library, supplied to Ruth Kelly

Valuing choice	
Policies	*Cost*
Parenting allowance/baby premium for first year of baby's life[4]	£770 million
Long maternity leave entitlement[5]	
• Extend flat-rate SMP payment to 52 weeks	£590 million
• Extend SMP at 90% of earnings to 26 weeks	£1.1 billion
Encouraging return to work part-time after time-off • reduced hours threshold in WFTC	[data currently unavailable]
Encouraging return to work part-time after time-off[6]	
• increased earnings disregard in Income Support to £30 a week for parents (all ages of children)	£50 million
• increased earnings disregard in Income Support to £30 a week for parents (at least one child under 5)	£12.5 million
• increased earnings disregard in Income Support to £37 (10 hours at minimum wage) a week for parents (at least one child under 5)	£60-£70 million
Unpaid parental leave/payment at a low level[7]	£175 million

4 Costings of £70 a week based on WFTC tapers for net income over £90 week – not including SMP recipients, from answer to Parliamentary Question, supplied to Ruth Kelly

5 Costings from answer to Parliamentary Question, supplied to Ruth Kelly

6 Costings from HoC Library, supplied to Ruth Kelly

7 13 weeks per parent paid at £100 a week. Take-up assumptions based on ICM poll (April 2000) on parental leave and costed by KPMG.

Of course, it might be that the Government tries to promote elements of each model – attempting to facilitate people's capacity to move between caring roles and full participation in the labour market. It might also be that greater emphasis is placed on one model or the other for people at different stages in the life-cycle – for example, greater emphasis on caring for those looking after very young children, as opposed to those whose children are of school age – or that different emphases are put on the Choice versus Parent-Citizen-Worker models in different family structures. It can, for instance, be argued that free choice for women can never be the overriding factor in policy design – as other influences, such as the welfare of children and the cost to the state of free choice, also have a legitimate influence on policy.

All the evidence suggests that children's welfare in terms of employment, educational and behavioural outcomes, is strongly influenced (in a positive sense) by the presence of a working role model in the household, while they are still at school. With the additional constraint that the free choice of lone parents costs the state far more in subsidy than that of a parent in a working household, the Government could argue for a Parent-Citizen-Worker model for lone parents with children over a certain age with relative ease, while favouring 'informed' choice and explicitly valuing caring – for one parent – in families headed by a couple. However, it is clear that exclusive concentration on one 'preferred' model of the family would be premature or counter-productive, or both.

References

Beck U (1992) *Risk Society: Towards a New Modernity* London: Sage.

Hakim C (1999) Models of the Family, Women's Role and Social Policy, A New Perspective from Preference Theory *European Societies* 1 (1): 33-58.

Harkness S *et al* (1995) *Evaluating the pin-money hypothesis, the relationship between women's labour market activity, family income and poverty in Britain* STICERD paper 108, London: LSE.

Labour Market Trends (1999) *Women in the Labour Market* London: Labour Market Trends, March.

Leira A (1998) 'Cash for Child Care and Daddy Leave' *Social Politics* Oxford: OUP.

Preference Theory *European Societies* 1 (1): 33-58.

SCB [Statistics Sweden] (1990/91} *Living Conditions* Stockholm: SBC.

IV: The Bigger Picture

15. Gender and the knowledge economy: work, family and e-business

Patricia Hewitt

As New Labour often says, the old politics required a choice between economic efficiency and social justice. The old left and the new right chose different sides, but both were agreed that the choice had to be made. For us, however, it is central that in the modern economy, the choice need not be made – indeed, it must not be made. Instead, the policies that are required in the interests of social justice – above all, the extension of opportunity to all – are precisely the same policies that are required to create a successful modern economy.

But of course it's not so simple. There are real tensions between egalitarian values, and the inegalitarian forces of the global economy. Social justice may be good for economic dynamism. But is economic dynamism good for social justice?

In this chapter, I shall look at one aspect of social justice – equality between women and men – and its relationship to the new economy.

The shift from an industrial to a post-industrial or knowledge-based economy at the beginning of the 21st century is quite as profound as the shift from an agricultural to an industrial economy was at the beginning of the 19th century...and the social upheavals are just as painful.

The new information and communications technologies, and the convergence of computing, telecommunications and broadcasting, are at the heart of the new economy. There is now pretty solid evidence from the US that convergence is driving down prices, driving up productivity and creating new jobs even faster than it destroys old ones.

The rate of change is almost impossible to grasp. Just one day's activity in 1999 was equivalent to :

- all world trade in 1949

- all scientific projects in 1960

- all telephone calls in 1983

- and all e-mails in 1990.

But I want to emphasise one particular feature of the knowledge-driven economy – the intensification of forces of inequality.

Growing inequality

First, there are growing returns to human capital. Young graduates earn, on average, about a third more than their non-graduate peers. By the time they reach their late

40s, graduates are earning 76 per cent more. In the US, a graduate premium of 46 per cent in 1980 has stretched to 75 per cent in 1998.

The recent study of women's lifetime incomes in the UK reveals that a childless woman with no educational qualifications could expect to earn £518,000 over her lifetime, compared with £650,000 for a woman with intermediate skills and nearly twice as much – £1,190,000 – for a graduate woman (Women's Unit, 2000).

Not only does better education improve women's lifetime earnings, but it reduces the financial impact of motherhood. Whereas the low-skill mother of two is estimated to forgo nearly 60 per cent of her potential earnings after childbirth, the high-skill mother (relying on paid childcare) loses on average only £20,000 or two per cent of her potential after-childbirth earnings.

The well-educated now do much better compared with the poorly educated – in access to jobs and in pay for the jobs they get – than they used to. Intelligence (in its many forms), creativity and education are increasingly important. But they are not evenly distributed, by nature or nurture.

Second, there is a widening gap between top and bottom incomes within each education group. The stars who play in the global marketplace command global incomes, whether they are lawyers, merchant bankers, footballers, pop stars or academics. Those who are only a bit less gifted – or a bit less lucky – get nothing like as much.

But this is not simply about individual talent or good fortune. The organisation matters too. The individual working for an outstandingly successful company – whether senior manager or secretary – will be far better rewarded than the senior manager or secretary, who is just as well qualified but works in an average or poorly-run firm.

Third, competition is intense. Liberalisation, global markets, the transparency of the Euro across eleven countries, and above all the instant availability of real-time information on digital networks are creating a powerfully – even harshly – competitive environment. That helps to improve productivity, but it also drives earnings closer to people's individual productivity and away from 'the rate for the job'. And there are good reasons, to do with fairness as well as incentives, for relating pay to performance. But as markets become more competitive, cross-subsidies of all kinds are unwound – including transfers from the more to the less productive.

Fourth, global capital and business are able to move wherever they will find the highest rewards. Governments have to compete for mobile investment. If taxes on business or individuals are too high, those who make corporate decisions will go elsewhere. And governments are thus constrained in their ability to raise resources to tackle inequality – whether directly through redistribution or indirectly through investment in wider opportunities.

Fifth, stock market growth, particularly in the US, is creating extraordinary capital gains for investors.

And, last but not least, the scale of disruption is vast. It is wrong to see the new economy as replacing manufacturing with services. Manufacturing is itself being transformed by the application of new technologies and new knowledge, so that the boundaries between services and manufacturing are increasingly blurred.

The old industries don't disappear in the knowledge economy. But their nature changes, and above all – as global competition intensifies – the old jobs disappear. We see the results in deteriorating health and rising crime and drug-taking in many once strongly-knit communities. There is some worrying evidence that it is in those very communities or even regions that were particularly dependent upon one or two industries, that employers find it most difficult to generate the new, smaller and more varied enterprises of the knowledge economy.

And the changes don't end with the disappearance of some of our old industries. They are a permanent feature of the new economy. Jobs are lost faster – and created faster. More businesses start – but the risk is that more businesses fail too. Instability is inherent in the speed of technological change. But intense change strains people's capacity to cope with change. And the most vulnerable are those with poor health, little money, out-of-date skills and low self-confidence.

These changes are happening world-wide. Not every advanced economy has seen the same increase in inequality. Indeed, it has been more extreme in the United Kingdom in the 1980s than almost anywhere else. The experience of both Germany and France suggest that successful economies can live with far less inequality than Britain or the US – and certainly, the United States is not the only model for the new economy. But the forces of inequality are powerful, and as the continental economies become more exposed to global stock markets, and to competition from the new economies of Central and Eastern Europe, it would be surprising if we didn't see some of the same results there too.

Men's and women's jobs in the new economy

In the US, where the new knowledge-driven economy is most advanced, its most striking feature has been sustained job creation. The view from the European left has been that these are merely 'MacJobs' – low-paid, insecure, dead-end. But that is simply not the case.

Low-skilled service jobs are just over one-fifth of US employment – a figure that has remained constant for the last 20 years. The biggest employment growth since 1993 has come in the highest-paid jobs. More than five million new jobs were created in five years in professional, executive and managerial positions. Indeed, by 2006, one third of all jobs are expected to require an associated degree or above. In the lowest-earnings group, the job growth has been over two million, and in the middle-earnings group only around 1.6 million – about enough to replace those lost between 1989 and 1993.

Here in the UK, with a much shorter period of stability behind us, unemployment has fallen to a 20-year low. Youth unemployment fell by nine per cent last year. Long-term unemployment by 13 per cent. And the number of people in work is higher than ever before.

All those fears of 'the end of work' seem rather dated now. We certainly shouldn't assume that the knowledge driven economy has to be short on jobs. Indeed, it is much more likely to suffer from a shortage of skilled and educated people.

The changing nature of the global economy – and, in particular, the shift from manufacturing to service sector jobs in countries like the UK – affects men and women differently. Fewer than one in five of all jobs are now in manufacturing, and most of the job losses have been in full-time employment previously dominated by men. Three-quarters of all jobs are now in services, and much of the job gain has been in part-time employment and in occupations dominated by women.

But the increased employment has come entirely among women with better educational qualifications. Whereas labour market activity among women with higher qualifications has continued to increase – from 78 per cent in 1984 to 86 per cent in 1998 – the rate has actually fallen among women with no qualifications, from 59 per cent to 50 per cent in the same period.

Looking at labour market trends, the Office of National Statistics projects that of the 1.7 million new jobs that will be created before 2011, some 1.4 million will be taken by women. With men's employment rates falling (from 91 per cent in 1971 to 84 per cent in 1998) and women's rising (from 57 per cent in 1971 to 72 per cent in 1998), women's employment is increasingly important to the country's economic health.

Furthermore, as Charles Leadbeater has stressed, the knowledge economy seems to flourish in a cosmopolitan culture that values individuals' talents regardless of their race, sex or class (Leadbeater, 2000). Creativity thrives upon diversity. The old inequalities – including the old English vice of class – have no place in a successful modern economy. So diversity has an economic – as well as an ethical – importance.

But the UK economy – and it is not alone in this – remains highly segregated. An OECD study estimated that, in 1995, 60 per cent of all British women were employed within the ten most feminised occupations, where 80 per cent of the workforce were female. In these occupations, the gap between men's and women's pay is even wider than in the economy as a whole.

It is, therefore, disturbing to find that women are under-represented in the new economy's lead sector, information and communications technology (ICT). Indeed, there is general agreement within the sector that fewer women are joining it than two decades ago. A recent report from the Government's Information Age Partnership confirms that one reason for the sector's growing skill shortages is that it recruits from only half the population.

In my own discussions with young entrepreneurs, I hear repeatedly that women are simply not interested in applying for technical or engineering jobs. Instead, they join the new businesses in creative, marketing and customer support roles. Even when they acquire extensive technical knowledge – as those in customer support rapidly do – they are often reluctant to be redefined as technicians, even when the technical jobs are better-paid.

The male image of ICT is unmistakable. Games arcades are full of boys. PC stores are overwhelmingly staffed by young men. Video and computer games are marketed and designed for male appeal. It is not surprising, therefore, that young women resist 'boys' toys' when making their own education and career choices, nor that women are much less likely to have or use a computer at home.

But there are some signs of change. Women are the fastest-growing group of Internet users, and health sites are increasingly popular (if not quite catching up with pornography). The Open University recently created a course on 'You and Your Computer' which attracted record proportions of women – and indeed proved so popular generally that it had to be repeated.

The challenge to teachers and course designers, as well as to employers and business, is to focus upon the content and the applications, rather than the underlying technologies. Otherwise, if ICT remains a male preserve, we will continue to be held back economically by a shortage of skilled people; computing applications will continue to be biased towards men; and women will miss out on well-paid technical opportunities.

Family policy

Profound changes in the labour market have been accompanied by – and are closely related to – changes in the family.

Families are the place where two kinds of inequality meet. The vertical inequality between richer and poorer – which is driven by the distribution of paid work. And the horizontal inequality between women and men – which is largely about the distribution of unpaid work.

Every family has a double responsibility. Families need to earn a living, and they need to care for their children. The post-war period saw a pretty settled distribution of those tasks, between men who earned the living, and women who cared for the children. It was never universal, but it was the majority experience and it exercised a powerful influence as an ideal. Indeed, the idea remains powerful, even when the reality has changed profoundly.

We all understand why the two-parent, single-earner family is now in the minority. Women's own aspirations and the dramatic increase in employment amongst better-educated women. The changing needs of a labour market where most jobs are in services. Longer life expectancy and smaller families. The rejection of religious and legal authority that used to enforce marriage by stigmatising illegitimacy and divorce.

As families have changed, however, there has been no new settlement between family and market. Balancing work and family – hardly an issue in the 1950s and 60s – is now a daily source of strain.

The conflict between work and family is still far more acute for mothers than for fathers. When we think of a 'good father', we still mainly think about earning a living, what used to be called 'being a good provider'. In fact, more and more fathers, too, are complaining that the demands of their work make it impossible to give their children and partners the time and attention they want. That's hardly surprising when the UK has the longest full-time working hours in the European Union.

But when we think of a 'good mother', we think of the mother spending time with her children. Many believe that, to fulfil their parental responsibilities properly, mothers have to leave employment altogether or work part-time. And at the moment, paid maternity leave, followed by part-time work, does seem to be the pattern that gives women the greatest satisfaction. But there is a price to pay. Although the pay gap between men and women persists even for women without children, it is very substantially increased for mothers who take long periods out from full-time employment.

The alternative – and it is one pursued by a growing proportion of women with children – is to work full-time and find substitute childcare, whether within the family or paid. In other words, they fit into working patterns that were organised on the assumption that the worker would have a wife to care for home and family. Not surprisingly, many women who are both worker and wife or partner find themselves torn between living up to the demands of the workplace for longer and longer hours, and living up to a domestic ideal of full-time motherhood, and feeling that in the end they are doing neither properly.

Full-time work for both parents also has implications for equality. The last twenty years has seen a growing divide between the work-rich family and the work-poor. Since most people choose their partners from within the same educational group, and since the best-educated find it easiest to get work, the work-rich are likely to be in the higher-skilled, better-paid jobs, with both parents working full-time. Meanwhile, the work-poor find themselves trapped by low skills, benefits barriers and limited local labour markets with casual and low-paid work or nothing at all. Worst off are the teenage, never-married mothers whose earnings are typically depressed by nearly 60 per cent compared even with the low-skilled childless woman.

For the best-educated women, the pay gap with men is shrinking and the pay penalty of motherhood is at its lowest. At the top, gender equality is greater, but inequality between top and bottom increases.

It is not for government to dictate to parents how they balance their responsibilities. But it is our job to widen parents' choice about how they do it. For those trapped outside employment, the priority is to support work. Hence the New Deal for lone parents, and for the partners of unemployed claimants. Increasingly, an effective anti-poverty strategy must build people's capacity to learn and to earn their way out of poverty – instead of simply trying to relieve poverty through the passive route of higher benefits. When the majority of the poor are women, tackling poverty – and improving the life-chances of children – demands sustained investment in new opportunities for women at every stage in their lives. But with employment rates falling for both men and women who lack educational qualifications, radical reform of the education system is essential both to provide the educated workforce that a growing knowledge economy demands, and to enable adults, and their children, to escape from unemployment and low pay.

At the same time, it is essential to help working parents get the time they need at home. Hence the Working Time Directive and the introduction of parental leave. And the Working Families Tax Credit – although its main purpose is, rightly, to make work pay – is also designed to support families in achieving a balance between paid and unpaid work. Because it provides a significant increase to a part-time wage – starting at 16 hours a week – it helps lone parents balance work and family. Because it includes a child care credit, it benefits families who need to pay for childcare. But for a two-parent family with a single earner, it equally enables one partner to care for the children at home.

I have indicated the stresses that the modern labour market can place on family life. We can't get rid of them all. But as well as the changes already made, we can see ways in which a more flexible labour market can help families balance their lives. As employers find it increasingly important – and difficult – to recruit and retain the people they want, they are reshaping working hours to meet people's needs. Several NHS hospitals offer nursing staff almost complete freedom to choose their hours, sometimes using time management software to match staff preferences with patients' needs. Small businesses often need heroic commitment from their staff – but offer flexibility for personal priorities in return. And new, Internet-enabled ways of working can produce surprising results. One leading-edge electronics firm that I met recently no longer has any offices or fixed hours at all. All their work is organised on the web, and their 'associates' – who used to be called their staff ! – bid for the work they want to do. When they do it is entirely up to them.

The fatherhood factor

But as we stress the importance of women earning a living, it is equally important to value the non-financial contribution that men make to their families. Equal opportunities in the workplace won't be secured without equal responsibilities at home. But women themselves may be quite ambivalent, or even hostile, about sharing responsibilities at home. In her ground-breaking book, *Fatherhood Reclaimed*,

Adrienne Burgess has written of the often subtle ways in which the new father can be de-skilled from the earliest days of the baby's life (Burgess, 1997).

Not surprisingly, the conflict is sharpest where the parents are separated or divorced. In my constituency advice surgeries, I see a growing number of fathers who are bitter at having to pay for children from whose lives they feel excluded. Even the father who is the parent with residence can struggle to get child benefit paid directly to him. Where the mother has residence, as most do, she may well feel that she wants nothing more to do with her former partner. But that will rarely be in the child's best interests. From the child's point of view, after all, every family is a two parent family.

Thirty years ago, we began to change the cultural and legal barriers that made it so hard for women to advance in the workplace, Now we have to change the cultural and legal barriers that make it so hard for men to spent time with their children. More employers are recognising a right to paternity leave. By giving fathers a separate entitlement to parental leave, we are helping to signal the importance of fathers' time to their children. And we are reforming the Child Support Agency, introducing a simple maintenance formula that most people should feel is fair. This provides for lower maintenance where the child lives with both parents and, above all, a clear understanding that support payments are only part of the close relationship and loving support that children need, wherever possible, from both father and mother.

Poverty makes for family disruption and exacerbates family dysfunction – though we shouldn't make the mistake of thinking that dysfunctional families are confined to the poor. The problem is not only poverty, and the solution is not only money. Indeed, the problems of families in trouble – which may include mental as well as physical illness, violence, alcohol and drug abuse, as well as child neglect – may be the cause of family poverty as well as an expression of it.

Families with these acute difficulties are, of course, a minority. But it is worrying that so many schools in low-income communities report that they are seeing more disturbed children, and more children who are disturbed at a very early age. Children, in other words, who simply aren't ready to learn because their basic needs – for emotional as well as material security – are not being met.

In my constituency, the head of one community college explained that they started seeing children in their creche – as young as eighteen months – who were already completely out of control. They created an early education partnership, bringing mothers and children together in playgroups. For many of the mothers, it was – as the group leader, herself a mother, said – 'the first time that they'd discovered how to play with their babies'.

That partnership is now a Sure Start programme. Sure Start is our flagship family programme, designed to offer every family within a disadvantaged community early contact with a supportive neighbour, before or soon after the baby is born. It will fill gaps in existing provision, whether that is through parent and toddler groups, or toy libraries, or family literacy programmes. Even more important, it is designed to bring together the statutory agencies – health, education, social services – in far more effective working partnerships.

Community empowerment and new markets

Families exist within communities – and children are more likely to thrive in strong and reasonably stable communities. For all the talk about Internet-enabled 'virtual' communities, place still matters. And investment in people needs to be matched by investment in places. But it cannot be the property-led investment of the last administration's attempts at urban renewal.

We know from experience here in Europe, in the US and in the developing world that sustainable local communities and economies cannot be created top-down. Government can't end social exclusion on its own; but nor can we leave it all to others. Instead, we need a new partnership of government, business, and the not-for-profit sector, the 'third sector' of community and voluntary groups.

That is the philosophy of the New Deal for Communities and the other area-based programmes – the Single Regeneration Budget, the Action Zones for Education, Health and Employment, and Sure Start. We are using the offer of substantial public investment to 'pull through' the development of resident-led partnerships. Not local councils or other statutory agencies deciding what is good for the community – and then going home at night. But local people coming together in what is often a very difficult process, to thrash out their own priorities and to create genuine partnerships with public agencies and private business to support those priorities.

Above all, we need the leadership of local people – and substantial investment in capacity-building to enable that leadership to emerge and deal powerfully with statutory agencies and other partners in renewal. As Bea Campbell has testified from her own experience and research, it is often women who are the leaders in community renewal, perhaps because they are most dependent upon place and upon public services, and most determined to do something to improve the future for their children (Campbell, 1993).

Because human capital is the prime source of wealth creation in the new economy, investment in human capital becomes an economic necessity rather than a social cost. Once a stable economic framework is secured, the way to grow the economy is to grow the labour force – literally, by drawing more and more people into employment, and metaphorically, by expanding the capacity and productivity of each person employed.

This is not so much wealth creation first, redistribution next – but redistribution through wealth creation. The result is that in the new economy, social and economic policies are no longer separate. Child-care, skill-building and community development are as much part of economic policy as managing interest rates and taxation. Diversity is a matter of economics as well as ethics. Equal opportunities is driven by business survival as much as individual needs. And any government that wants our country to succeed in the knowledge-driven economy must open up opportunities to women and men, challenge the segregation of roles in both the workplace and the home. Indeed, the central aim of all domestic policy must be to build the capacity of individuals and families, communities and businesses – the capacity to survive and to thrive, both economically and socially.

References

Burgess A (1997) *Fatherhood Reclaimed* London: Vermillion.

Campbell B (1993) *Goliath* London: Methuen.

Leadbeater C (2000) *Living on Thin Air* London: Penguin.

Women's Unit (2000) *Women's Income over the Lifetime* London: Cabinet Office.

16. Well women and medicine men: gendering the health policy agenda
Anna Coote and Liz Kendall

Health and healthcare are profoundly affected by sex and gender differences. Indeed, there are few aspects of human health or of any conventional healthcare system that are not experienced differently by men and women or shaped by physical or social differences between them.

Right across the spectrum, from bodily functions and personal behaviour, through morbidity and mortality rates, to attitudes to disease and medicine, patterns of demand for services, and employment in health-related professions, there are significant differences in the ways in which women and men do things and have things done to them. But there is nothing simple about this. In strikingly similar ways, gender and health are both products of a complex interplay of biological and shifting social, economic and environmental factors. Public policy is much better informed now than it was – say – ten years ago about the construction of gender and of health. Inevitably, though, understanding has developed in fits and starts and remains unevenly distributed in opinion-forming and policy-making circles. It is still common to hear leading politicians, health care professionals and media commentators conflate health with the National Health Service, as though dealing with the 'crisis in the NHS' were really the only way to solve the nation's health problems. Just as often, similar voices are heard addressing the problem of 'teenage pregnancy' in terms that suggest girls achieve it singlehandedly, or discussing the 'family responsibilities' of employees as though they had nothing to do with men.

The comparison cannot be pushed too far. One important difference is that health – as opposed to health care – has always been on the policy agenda. Its ranking in the hierarchy has varied but only for the last half-century has it been treated as a second order issue. Gender has, until relatively recently, been overlooked or uncontested, except in the margins of political debate. Gender politics run much deeper in society than do the politics of science, clinical autonomy and welfarism that have combined to promote the cause of health services above that of the nation's health and well-being. In both cases, though, there are conflicts of interest and imbalances of power that serve to downplay or disempower one 'side' in favour of the other. And it is gradually becoming more widely recognised that this ultimately has negative consequences for both. If public policy fails adequately to prevent ill-health, to promote better health and to tackle health inequalities between different groups in the population, the National Health Service must pick up the increasingly expensive pieces. If public policy persists in assuming that gender roles are simple and satisfactorily fixed, men as well as women will find their opportunities unfairly limited and their quality of life seriously impaired.

In this chapter we argue, with health as our example, that a one-dimensional or over-simplified view of gender will distort policy and practice. In order to be relevant and effective, decision-making requires a sophisticated understanding of the multiple determinants of health and the shifting complexities of gender, as well as the relationships between health and gender – and how these bear upon the changing dynamics of power within the health sector. We look first at how ideas about gender and health have developed since the 1970s, and at some of the differences between women's and men's health and their relationship with health services. We then consider the lessons for health policy.

Ideas about health and gender

The relationship between gender and health did not become explicit in mainstream political or sociological discourse until the 1970s. The orthodoxy, until then, was that health was a matter of biology, gender a natural phenomenon and medicine inevitably a male preserve. Men of science fought gladiatorial battles against disease within the human body, over which they ranged as if by right. Health was the product of victory in battle and patients – male and female – were the passive beneficiaries. Feminists challenged the orthodoxy, asserting women's ownership of their bodies, the value of their experiential knowledge, the fallibility of the medical establishment, and their right to participate in their own health care on their own terms (Phillips and Rakusen, 1996). The new women's movement campaigned for access to effective birth control, including abortion, and for more female-friendly health care and maternity services.

At the same time, feminist researchers had begun to trace links between women's ill-health and the unequal distribution of power and opportunity between women and men. By the late 1970s a new paradigm had emerged that emphasised the social construction of gender, the impact of gender on health, the differences between men's and women's healthcare requirements, and the need to focus on the specifics of women's health (Hunt and Annandale 1999, Annandale and Hunt, 2000).

Relatively simple connections were made at first between aspects of women's health and their subordination in a patriarchal system. It was argued, for example, that women were disadvantaged by the fact that the male-dominated medical professions overlooked or misunderstood their health problems and/or treated them as second-class patients; if women were treated more like men, they would enjoy better health services and eventually better health.

But over the next two decades a more sophisticated analysis took shape. This was heavily influenced by feminists as well as by proponents of the 'new public health' who insisted on a holistic view of health and its determinants (Ashton and Seymour 1998). Broadly, it sought to understand gender in the context of race, ethnicity and social class, and health as a product of the interplay between biological, psycho-social, economic and environmental factors (Bird and Rieker 1999). It acknowledged shifting patterns of influence – within and between groups, and across the life cycle. It took more interest in gender comparisons, rather than targeting women's health and eventually the specifics of *men*'s health became a new focus of concern. In 1992, the Chief Medical Officer's Annual Report drew attention to differences between male and female morbidity and mortality rates (Department of Health, 1993). In 1994 the Royal College of Nursing established a Men's Health Forum, promoting the case for more and better health services for men.

Men's and women's health

Once the spotlight had shifted, it was hard to imagine how men's health had failed to attract attention. Men were dying, on average, five years younger than women. Boys born in 1996 could expect to live to 75, compared with 80 for women (Equal Opportunities Commission 1998). Between the ages of 20 and 24, vehicle accidents and suicides helped to drive up the male death rate to nearly three times the rate for women. Across the whole of adult life, death rates were higher for men than for women for all the major causes of death, including cancer and cardiovascular disease (Acheson 1998).

Some (notably in the misogynist school of journalism) have argued that, in asserting women's health needs, feminism has distorted the picture and eclipsed the more serious needs of men. A more defensible argument is that the case for men's health would not have been made at all if feminists had not put gender on the policy map. This prompted men (and women) to investigate masculinities and how these are shaped by social and economic circumstances. This, in turn, is beginning to shed some light on why men die younger than women and what might help to safeguard their health.

Gender is now, so to speak, out in the open. But how much is known about the specifics of men's and women's experiences of health and health care, and the differences between them? There is certainly a wealth of information, but it often seems to beg more questions than it answers. Many of the changes in men's and women's lives and life choices are not captured by statistics. All we can do in this short chapter is to offer some visible evidence of the range of contradictions and uncertainties that prevail. Broadly, these fall into four categories: mortality and morbidity rates; health-related behaviours; patterns of health service use and employment and status in the National Health Service.[1]

Mortality and morbidity

- Overall life expectancy has increased for both sexes over the last century and a half, but the gap between them has grown. Between 1841 and 1991, male life expectancy increased from 41 to 73, while female life expectancy increased from 43 to 79. Only recently has the gap begun to narrow very slightly.

- Poverty and ill-health are closely related. Women's income over lifetime is significantly lower than men's. Yet, using the Townsend index as a measure of deprivation, the least well off women have lower mortality rates than the most well off men.

- Boys appear to have higher rates of chronic physical illness in childhood, as well as higher rates of psychological disorder. This pattern is reversed in early-to-mid adolescence, when rates for both are higher for girls.

- Women suffer more from poor mental health, especially from anxiety and depressive disorders. Lone mothers are particularly prone to ill-health, even after controlling for household income, employment status and occupation. However, men are a lot more likely to commit suicide, especially in young adulthood.

- While women can expect to live five years longer than men, their expectation of a healthy life is only 2-3 years longer. Fewer than one in five men over 85 are unable to go out and walk down the road, compared with nearly one in two women in the same age group.

- It has been claimed that 'men and women have different perceptions of their own and each others' health' (Lloyd 1996). While men and women have similar concepts of health, both see men as healthier. Men stress being fit, strong, energetic, physically active and being in control, while women stress not being ill and never seeing a doctor (Saltonstall R). Men are more likely see exercise as more important than food and rest, whilst women see food, rest and then exercise as important (Blaxter 1990).

- Recent research examined the differences among men and among women (rather than between them) in how they rated their own health. When they were sorted by social class, gender appeared to make no difference. But when education was used instead of class as a measure of socio-economic status, the study found greater inequality among men at age 33 for limiting long-standing illness and respiratory symptoms, but greater inequality among women for poor rated health at age 23 and psychological distress at age 33.

Health related behaviour

- Men appear to take more risks with their health (through sport, through dangerous or violent activities and, classically, through war). Young men are much more likely to die from an accident than young women: 40 per cent of premature deaths among 16-24-year-old men are due to accidents, compared with 24 per cent for women in the same age group. Yet accidental death is associated with lower socio-economic status and, when measured by employment status, as it usually is, low socio-economic status is more common among young women than young men (Colhoun and Prescott-Clarke 1996).

- Men are more likely to drink than women, and to drink more. In 1997 27 per cent of men drank more than 21 units per week, while only 14 per cent of women drank more than 14 units. However, the proportion of 18-24 year old women drinking more than 14 units a week has risen from 15 per cent in 1984 to 24 per cent in 1996. Drinking rates among professional women have also risen during this period.

- The proportion of 15-year-old girls who smoke has risen from 22 per cent in 1988 to 33 per cent in 1996. But overall, men still smoke more than women (30 per cent compared with 27 per cent of women) and smoking rates have recently increased among younger men aged 16 to 34 – from 33 per cent in 1993 to 39 per cent in 1996. (Department of Health, 1998.)

- Men are more likely to be overweight than women, (45 per cent compared with 34 per cent), but women are more likely to be obese (18 per cent compared with 16 per cent). Weight also varies by social class, with men and women in manual occupations more likely to be obese or overweight than those in professional groups.

Patterns of health service use

- Boys are between 30 and 40 per cent more likely than girls to have consulted their GP for a serious condition, but 10 per cent less likely to have done so for a minor illness.

- Women are more likely to consult their GP than men, particularly under the age of 45. In 1996-7, one in five women aged 16-44 had consulted their GP in the fortnight prior to their interview with the General Household survey, compared with one in 10 men in the same age group. The proportion of men and women consulting their GP has increased since 1971, but the increase has been greater among women.

- It is widely assumed that women are more ready than men to report illness and to seek help. Men – by contrast – are thought to be reluctant visitors to surgeries. So when they do go, their complaints are somehow presumed to have a more serious content. But this is not supported by evidence, according to Professor Sally Macintyre, of the Medical Research Council (MRC) social and public health sciences unit, in Glasgow. Her analysis of data from the MRC's common cold unit has shown that men 'over-rate' their sniffles, sore throats, headaches, and shivers compared with ratings given by clinical observers, while women under-rate their symptoms (McKie 2000).

- Although older women are substantially more likely to experience functional impairment in mobility and personal self-care than men of the same age, there is little difference between women and men in their reporting of self-assessed health and limiting longstanding illness – regardless of marital status, social class, income and housing tenure.

- When a group of 192 doctors examined male and female actors playing the part of patients suffering identically from chest pains and shortness of breath, they were much more likely to arrive at a cardiac diagnosis in men, and to rate women as suffering from emotional problems and recommend psychiatric treatment (McKie 2000).

Employment in health services

- Women account for 33 per cent of hospital doctors, 31 per cent of GPs and 21 per cent of consultants. Their share of jobs in health professions has increased significantly in the last 10 years. In 1998, women accounted for 56 per cent of the new intake into medical school. But they remain under-represented among surgeons (less than five per cent) and among senior consultants in all fields. (Millar 2000)

- Nursing, health visiting, midwifery and community nursing are predominantly female professions.

Lessons for health policy

The evidence suggests a complex and often contradictory picture. Men and women have different health experiences, but these are changing as men's and women's social and economic circumstances change, and are not always in line with prevailing assumptions about gender differences. The causes of health and ill-health clearly need to be sought beneath the surface of official statistics, in the shifting relationships between social change and individual choice. For example, very little of the data about different male and female mortality rates are adequately explained. If policy-makers are serious about tackling inequalities in health, this needs much more careful consideration.

Men and women may react differently – and in ways that may affect their mental or physical health – to different conditions. Adolescence appears to bring more risk of psychological disorder to females more than to males, with consequences for the physical health of young women (Sweeting 1994). There are conventions of masculinity that affect the way men regard their bodies and risk taking, making them more prone to accidents and injury and more careless about the adverse effects of behaviour on their health. 'The ideal male body suffers no pain or weakness, is never ill and never breaks down...[but if it does] This experience may even challenge a man's sense of his masculinity... In discourses on masculinity it is often suggested that to be a man is to invite, rather than to avoid, risk.' (Petersen and Lupton, 1996)

Unemployment may be more of a blow to self-esteem for men in their early 20s than for women – at least as long as the tradition of men being the family breadwinner persists. Young women can derive a sense of purpose and an adult identity from early parenthood. But young men who don't have jobs (or jobs that mean anything to them) have to earn their rites of passage to adulthood in other ways, often depending more heavily on their peers and on 'proving' themselves through risky or challenging behaviour (Coote 1993).

Michael Marmot's much-quoted Whitehall studies have indicated an important link between health and the extent to which people feel in control of their lives. He found that ill-health had less to do with income or one's place in the workplace hierarchy, than with the relationship between the levels of demand put on individuals and how far they can control their own work and its outcomes (van Rossum *et al* 2000). Power and control are available to men and women – and hold meaning for them – in different ways. Not just at work, but in the rest of life too. This affects the distribution of resources which, in turn, may affect the quality of individuals' lives and their sense of well-being,

So in understanding the causes of ill-health, we need to consider how social and economic change affects gender and how changing gender roles affect health. As paid employment becomes more significant to the identity of women, will that mean that unemployment carries a greater health risk for them? If men play a greater role in parenting, deriving from it an enhanced sense of purpose and identity, could that mean that they would find it easier to cope with spells of unemployment? As lone parenthood becomes more commonplace and less stigmatised, is it less likely to be correlated with ill-health in women? Or is the fact that lone mothers are considered a deviant social model less detrimental to health than the burden of bringing up children alone?

These are all things that need to be better understood in order to tackle inequalities in health and to improve the health of men and women. There are now some experimental health improvement strategies that are designed to reach men through their masculinity. 'Alive and Kicking', for example, is a Midlands-based health outreach project organised around amateur football teams. The aim is to raise awareness of health issues with young men, and help them develop healthier lifestyles, using a multi-agency approach.

But there are dangers in oversimplifying the picture. One danger is that health improvement strategies will entrench gender stereotyping (for example, underscoring the message that competitive sport is a 'manly' pursuit). Another danger is that the differences *among* men and *among* women will be overlooked. That is why we need a complex understanding not only of the multiple determinants of health, and of the multiple components of gender – but also of the interaction between gender and other factors, including ethnicity, education, employment, income and environment.

As Macintyre and others have commented, the view that women experience more ill health but on average die later than men has become so well-entrenched that 'over-generalisation has become the norm, with inconsistencies and complexities in patterns of gender differences in health being overlooked. In the face of an apparently clear pattern, there has been a tendency to downplay (or maybe not even to report) data that conflict with rather than confirm the general pattern'. (Macintyre, Hunt and Sweeting, 1999).

This complex analysis is important not only for understanding why men and women get ill and how they might improve their health, but also, as we have seen, for accurate diagnosis and treatment. If clinicians make stereotyped assumptions about the diseases to which men and women are prone, or about male and female patterns of interpreting and reporting symptoms, they could do more harm than good. Women suffering from heart disease are evidently vulnerable to misdiagnosis. More generally, if the notion of women as neurotic or hysterical complainers persists, then it is more likely that their complaints will be underrated by clinicians.

Equally important is the relationship between patterns of employment of men and women in the health service and the character and quality of treatment and care – and health policy more generally. There is still a significant gender divide within the health services and there is some evidence that this affects health outcomes. One study showed that general practices with female doctors, young doctors or more practice nurses had lower rates of teenage pregnancy (Hippisley-Cox et al 2000). The attitudes of clinicians and the quality of their relationships with service users are likely to be influenced by gender, age and ethnicity because their professional behaviour and judgements inevitably draw on their personal experience as well as their training. Their attitudes and relationships can, in turn, elicit a more or less positive response from service users, making their interventions more, or less, effective.

Most of the leading positions in the NHS are occupied by men. By and large they control the Department of Health, the NHS Executive, the major hospitals, most health authorities, almost all of the prestige specialist units in acute care and the all-important Royal Colleges, except the Royal College of Nursing. The President of one of the Royal Colleges was heard at a London seminar in 2000 to refer to the Minister for Public Health (Yvette Cooper) as 'What's her name – that little girl.'[2] We should not become so dazzled by the shifting nature of gender relations that we overlook the way in which male hegemony and an unreconstructed masculine view of the world prevail in the upper echelons of health policy and health care. Men still rule and it is *not* okay.

Traditional structures outlive the circumstances that created them: they defend sectional interests by helping to stave off the adjustments that are needed to work constructively with change. This may help to explain why it has been so difficult to shift priorities away from the 'battle against disease' towards a more holistic approach which puts health improvement, prevention, mental health and care of long-tem chronic conditions higher up the agenda. It may help to explain why power and the lion's share of resources, remain – in spite of much political rhetoric to the contrary – with the traditionally prestigious areas of acute healthcare. It certainly helps to explain why it has taken so long for nurses to play a bigger role in general practice. And why informal carers (usually grandmothers, mothers or daughters) – who in fact provide the backbone of healthcare – have been having such a hard time gaining recognition and a voice in shaping services.

Arguably, it also helps to explain why New Labour's public health agenda is so fixated on disease-based targets. Traditional forms of audit and evaluation, such as epidemiological studies and randomised control trials are a product and property of the traditional scientific establishment. They belong at the top of a 'hierarchy of evidence' by which other methods (such as observation, narrative and the views of service users) are judged inferior. Though invaluable for some purposes, they are less helpful in appraising strategies aimed at influencing the subtler, long-term developments in culture and social relations that are needed to address the root causes of ill health and inequality. At a time of diminishing confidence in scientific expertise, a strong focus on controlled evaluation can help to fend off public distrust. But traditional methodologies exert a powerful restraint on innovation and change. Policies that cannot be tested in a controlled environment, or that otherwise fail to produce easily measurable results, are regarded with suspicion. Decision-makers committed to 'evidence based medicine' and 'evidence based' policies would rather focus on what can be counted – such as the numbers of 'preventable deaths' from specific causes. This is one reason why the goal of developing 'healthy neighbourhoods' set out in New Labour's public health Green Paper *Our Healthier Nation*, gave way to goals aimed at reducing mortality rates in the subsequent White Paper, *Saving Lives*. The latter keeps health policy safely inside the traditional territory of professional medicine. The former is a messier objective, with multiple components, no scientific methods to rely upon and far less predictable outcomes. It requires the involvement of communities – and that means devolving power. As Bea Campbell has pointed out, women play a central role in communities, especially in deprived areas (Campbell, 1993). If the goal of healthier neighbourhoods is to be pursued, public sector institutions, including the NHS, need to understand the way women experience the world, in order to engage effectively with them. And they must be prepared to share power with them – not as patients but as partners in the production of better health. There are some promising examples of women leading innovations in local health improvement – such as the 'community mothers' scheme in Sparkbrook, Birmingham. But so far these are marginal to government health policy, which remains preoccupied with successive crises in acute care.

It would be facile to suggest that change is being resisted because men still dominate health policy-making. Many defenders of tradition in the health sector are female. Many advocates of the new health agenda are male. More to the point, the same historical factors that encouraged the emergence of feminism in the latter 20th century have undermined the orthodoxies of the medical world. The infallibility of science, the plausibility of a paternalistic, cradle-to-grave welfare state and the Victorian model of gender relations have all been challenged over the same period. Each challenge has a different dynamic, but all reflect – and owe their potency to – the same interplay of social and economic developments. Broadly, they arise because society has become more individualised and commodified, and because men and women are better educated, have a wider range of choices in how they live and are more inclined to want to decide for themselves, rather than be told what to do. As communications technologies and economic power become increasingly globalised, there is a growing awareness of risks affecting individuals, organisations, nations and the entire planet, which traditional political and professional institutions are manifestly ill-equipped to manage. All this has profound implications for the way decisions are made and implemented, in health and in other sectors. Individuals and organisations are having to negotiate new ways of living with uncertainty and change. Consequently, relations are changing between doctors and patients, between policy-makers and citizens and between men and women.

The same forces that have enabled women – and, more recently, men – to challenge assumptions about gender roles also impel them to question received wisdom about medicine and government, and to distrust experts and politicians who claim to know what is best for them. This is not a temporary blip in human behaviour, but a sea-change in the way society works and how it seeks and accommodates change. Policy makers must work with new patterns of attitude and behaviour. Traditional lines of authority are frayed to breaking point. Top-down instruction will have to give way to dialogue and reciprocal learning, with the internet playing an increasingly significant role. New weight must be given to the 'lay expertise' of those who experience illnesses, therapies and health services at first hand. Responsibility for change and attendant risks must be shared between individuals, community-level groups and organisations, and different layers of government.

Strikingly, both the green paper *Our Healthier Nation* and the subsequent white paper, *Saving Lives*, have called for a new, three-way 'contract' between the individual, the 'community' and national government – an approach that appears characteristic of 'third way' thinking. If any such 'contract' is to be effective, then the partners must have a clear view of each others' strengths and weaknesses, and how they can contribute, separately and together, to health improvement. Government will need to open itself up so that it can be better understood. It must acknowledge the complex ways in which social and economic circumstances, as well as gender, age and ethnicity, influence the behaviour of individuals and groups. It must use the resources of the state to build the capacity of individuals and groups to play their part to the full. And it must be prepared to share power with those it cannot directly control.

However, more traditional currents inside national government and the NHS are pulling in contrary directions. These favour professional hierarchies, cling to assumptions about medicine as a magic bullet and seek safety in policies that have measurable outputs. Their protagonists want change – a 'modern, dependable' NHS – but see change as best achieved by consolidating power at the centre, giving local leadership to one kind of doctor (general practitioners) at the expense of others (hospital consultants), and improving systems of management to speed up treatment, use beds more efficiently and reduce waiting lists. They are lukewarm about empowering patients and citizens because that cuts across their desire to centralise control. They are generally at ease in a system run by white middle class men and find the politics of gender and difference uncongenial. Traditional reformers of this kind are more powerful in Blairite circles than the more radical proponents of power-sharing and health strategies built from the bottom up. The 'third way' is sufficiently elastic to accommodate them, but they act as a brake on progress towards health improvement and greater health equality because they insist on the primacy of the NHS agenda, which is more about illness than health. Thus, while men are not responsible as such for resisting change, gender is an important part of the picture. More men than women derive power and status from the health system as it stands and therefore have an interest in defending the status quo. Paradoxically, it does not appear to be doing them any favours in terms of their life expectancy. A shift away from tradition, towards a broader and more innovative agenda, may be good for their health as well as for women's.

Conclusion

We set out to consider why gender should be of interest to those involved in health policy. First and foremost, it matters for reasons of equity in health. If health policy-makers are committed to reducing inequalities, then the fact that men die younger than women must be taken into account. There is an urgent need to know more about why people are healthy and why they get ill and how the health of men and women are affected differently by their different (and similar) life experiences.

Secondly, if policy-makes are committed to making health care more appropriate and effective, then they must take account of the different needs of men and women that are due to biological as well as social-economic factors, and to the ways in which the attitudes and behaviour of healthcare practitioners and their relationships with patients are influenced by gender.

Thirdly, gender is embedded in the politics of health. Those trying to change priorities – for example, by shifting resources towards tackling the root causes of illness – need to understand why change is required (or, indeed, inevitable) and why it is resisted. On both counts, a gendered analysis is helpful.

That said, a great deal depends on how gender is taken into account in each of these fields of interest.. A stereotyped view of gender is as likely to distort policy and practice as is the more traditional tendency of 'gender-blindness'. What matters is acknowledging the complexities of gender and how roles and identities change over time – and how, in turn, these affect health, its determinants, health care and health policy.

Endnotes

1   Except where specifically referenced, data in the rest of this section are taken from Acheson, 1998; Equal Opportunities 1998 and *Social Science and Medicine* (48), 1999.

2   Author's observation.

References

Acheson D (1998) *Report of the Independent Inquiry into Inequalities in Health* London: Stationery Office.

Annandale E and Hunt K (2000) *Gender Inequalities and Health* Buckingham: Oxford University Press.

Ashton J and Seymour H (1998) *The New Public Health* Oxford University Press, Oxford.

Bird CE and Rieker PP (1999) 'Gender matters: an integrated model for understanding men's and women's health' in *Social Science and Medicine* 48, 745-755.

Blaxter M (1990) *Health and Lifestyles* London:Tavistock/Routledge

Campbell B (1993) *Goliath* London: Methuen.

Colhoun H and Prescott-Clarke P (1996) in Department of Health, *Health Survey for England, 1994* London: Stationery Office.

Coote A (ed) (1993) *Families, Children and Crime* London: IPPR.

Equal Opportunities Commission, 1998, *Social Focus on Women and Men* Office for National Statistics, London: Stationery Office.

Department of Health (1993) *On the State of the Public Health 1992: The Annual Report of the Chief Medical Officer* London: Stationery Office.

Hippisley-Cox J *et al* (2000) 'Association between teenage pregnancy rates and the age and sex of general practitioners: cross sectional survey in Trent 1994-7) *British Medical Journal* 320, 842-5.

Hunt K and Annandale E (1999) 'Relocating gender and morbidity: examining men's and women's health in contemporary Western societies' in *Social Science and Medicine* 48, 1-5.

Lloyd T (1996) *Men's Health Review* Prepared on behalf of the Men's Health Forum, Royal College of Nursing.

Macintyre S, Hunt K and Sweeting H (1996) 'Gender differences in health: are things really as simple as they seem?' in *Social Science and Medicine* 42, 617-642.

McKie R (2000) 'Moaning men push women to back of the health queue' *The Observer* 7 May, 8.

Millar B (2000) 'Not there yet' *Health Service Journal* 17 February, 24-7.

Petersen A and Lupton D (1996) *The new public health: health and self in the age of risk* London: Sage.

Phillips A and Rakusen J (1996, revised edition) *The New Our Bodies Ourselves* (British edition) London: Penguin.

Saltonstall R (1993) 'Healthy Bodies, Social Bodies: Men's and Women's Concepts and Practices of Health in Everyday Life' *Social Science and Medicine* 36 (1), 7 – 14.

Social Science and Medicine (Special Edition) 48, 1999.

Sweeting H (1994) 'Reversals of fortune? Sex differences in health in childhood and adolescence' in *Social Science and Medicine* 40, 77-90.

van Rossum C T M, Shipley M J, van de Mheen H, Grobbee D E, Marmot M G (2000) 'Employment grade differences in cause specific mortality. A 25-year follow up of civil servants from the first Whitehall study' *Journal of Epidemiology and Community Health* 54, 178-184

17. The personal is political (again): a new politics of quality of life

Ian Christie and Michael Jacobs

There are good reasons to believe that the politics of the West is changing significantly, with political commitment and conflict 'migrating' to a new terrain – that of quality of life. This flows from the hollowing out of conventional politics after the end of the Cold War and of ideological confrontation over economic management, and from the parallel developments of globalisation and a growing recognition that there are limits to present forms of consumption and personal choice. A new politics of quality of life gives fresh energy to an old idea associated with environmentalism and feminism – that the 'personal is political' – and opens up new issues where these movements can form alliances. It focuses on the public implications of private wants and the impact of the social realm on key private goods – above all, on family time. It offers a new vocabulary and agenda for the articulation of classic problems and grievances over distribution associated with 'old style' ideological politics. But it also indicates a major weakness for the new politics – its lack of institutions through which new choices and priorities can find a voice and be translated into action.

The hollowing-out of politics

With the end of the Cold War a decade ago, there was a revival of the idea that the West was experiencing 'the end of ideology'. Certainly the collapse of Communism did much to give credence to the idea that ideological competition and passionate struggle in politics were reaching their end (Fukuyama, 1992). In the parts of the rich world where market forces had triumphed and a majority of citizens were classified as affluent, politics would be reduced to mild contests between pragmatic politicians seeking to manage capitalism better than their rivals.

There are good reasons to doubt that millennial capitalism in its Anglo-American form has put some kind of 'end' to history and ideology. In the 1990s the economic recessions in the West, the growing divisions between the rich and the poorest groups, and the soaring rewards available to business leaders and winners in the 'winner-take-all' markets of sport and entertainment, have all damaged the public image of big businesses (Frank and Cook, 1995). We cannot rule out a revival of forms of socialism and old ideological confrontations if Western economies enter a prolonged slump.

But for the moment – and it may be a long moment – politicians and many analysts of politics are acting as if the thesis of the 'end of history and ideology' were true. The battles between parties and personalities in the West, above all in the US, mask a deep consensus about the management of the economy and the primacy of growth and market-led innovations. Politicians have converged on the idea that their main goal is to run the economy so that citizens – conceived of essentially as consumers – can increase their spending power and choice:

> Today raising the level of consumer spending is generally regarded as the key political objective for any government: the principal measure of its success and – according to the conventional wisdom of psephological prediction – the best indicator of its likely vote (Jacobs, 1997).

Jacobs goes on to relate this to the impoverished debate in the UK on taxation: the Conservative governments of 1979-97 successfully embedded the idea in public discourse that tax is in all respects a 'burden', and that in particular income tax cuts provide people with more of 'their own money' to spend. Notwithstanding the advent of a Labour government, raising income tax has become a taboo idea in UK politics and similar developments are evident in the US and in continental Europe.

What stems from these changes is a 'hollowing out' of politics, as convergence on pragmatic economic management and laissez-faire approaches to business takes the confrontation out of major areas of policy, and as politicians deprive themselves of the fiscal means to make radical advances in tackling key issues – the worst examples of poverty, say, or the shortage of housing for the poorest groups in society. As JK Galbraith warned after the end of the Cold War, a largely affluent and middle-class society could become a 'culture of contentment' in which little or no action is taken to improve the lot of the electorally insignificant poor (Galbraith, 1992).

Galbraith's prognosis has been partially borne out. Even in the UK, with a Labour Government applying huge intellectual effort to the analysis of 'social exclusion' and setting itself ambitious targets for overcoming the worst cases of poverty and exclusion, debate on the divisions within society is played out sotto voce. Whatever we do to redistribute wealth is done 'by stealth', via indirect taxation and complex schemes to re-engage the 'excluded' with the world of work. Whatever we say about the evils of poverty, we cannot mention raising income tax, the most progressive of levies, or finding ways to limit growing inequalities of income. Nor do we have a political class, anywhere in the West, which is committed to promoting a challenging debate about the wider purposes of society and the moral dimension of the choices we make.

But the hollowing out of mainstream political debate does not signal the end of politics, even if it does point to the exhaustion of old institutions and processes no longer attuned to the attitudes, technologies and values abroad in hyper-modern societies. Far from it: the rise of affluence and the world of globalising markets which have both contributed to the demise of old political divisions are generating a new field of conflict and innovation.

'Life politics' emerge

The new terrain – in the affluent West – is that of *the politics of quality of life*. The key contests on this political ground concern the limits to present forms of consumption, the sources of satisfaction and meaning, and the relationship between personal choice and collective well-being. As Anthony Giddens has argued, the decline of older forms of ideological politics and the rise of mass affluence lead to a rediscovery of questions about personal purpose and ethical values. In his words, we see a new form of 'life politics' emerging (Giddens, 1991).

Politics is 'migrating' to this terrain in much of the affluent world. It may not stay there: a major economic slump could spark a renewal of the supposedly outmoded politics of class division and conflicts between market forces and state power. But for the moment, and for the foreseeable future if economic prosperity is maintained for the affluent majority, the direction of politics is away from the traditional lines and institutions of political debate and confrontation. The draining away of trust and interest from conventional politics and the growth in support for single-issue campaigns and NGO-based activism, especially among the young, is a key sign of this shift. Politics is not dying out, it is moving to new ground. And that ground is being staked out by individuals, NGOs, alliances of campaigning organisations, and community groups.

What is the content of the politics of quality of life? The issues from which it draws its energy and exerts its diffuse and often poorly articulated influence on society are precisely those which conventional politics refuses or finds it uncomfortable to address. Votes are still won – or thought to be won – on the basis of the traditional measures of economic growth and gains in spending power: *It's the economy, stupid*, as Bill Clinton's campaign teams never tired of saying. But the lesson of opinion polling in the 1990s is that there is no longer a straightforward connection between the mainstream economic indicators and the public's sense of the quality of everyday life. The 'feelgood factor' among the UK electorate conspicuously failed to revive on cue along with economic growth in the mid 1990s. There is a gap between what the economy delivers and what ever more people see as the important things in their lives.

In this gap, the politics of quality of life finds its expanding niche. The factors which dominate it are to do with both private goods and public ones. The key private good at stake is, increasingly, time: surveys have highlighted the extent to which 'time squeeze' and tensions between private time use (family life, friendship) and public time (workplace demands). But quality of life also depends on public goods as well as private ones. Much debate on quality of life has focused on the public realm where our choices and desires as consumers and private individuals rub against our preferences as workers and citizens. (Mulgan and Wilkinson 1995; Henley Centre 1997; Wilkinson 2000; Burchell 1999.)

There are certain issues that cannot easily be addressed by a politics of economic consensus that gives primacy to consumer choice and individual consumption. Chief among these are the conflicting demands of home life and the workplace, and the tension between political suport for a 'flexible' labour market and also for stronger and more stable family life. They include the environmental and social consequences of consumption choices, the ethical implications of rising affluence and consumption of resources from the developing world, and the purposes of economic development, scientific research and technical innovation.

Before examining these areas it is worth considering the place of 'quality of life' as an item in political and economic discourse. The extent to which quality of life concerns have begun to shape mainstream political debate and policy ideas is indicated by an emerging critique of conventional economic measurement and political priorities, and particularly the inadequate attention they pay to qualitative notions of well-being. 'Quality of life' is a concept which goes well beyond the reach of conventional economic measures. Politicians and economists still focus most attention on living standards and GDP growth rates, and on the inputs and outputs of the economy. Obviously, vast realms of activity and meaningful 'value-added' are routinely left out: the 'love economy' of informal care, the quality of services experienced by citizens, the texture of daily life, the quality of social relations, the fabric of the towns and the quality of the natural environment, and more besides. When we reflect on what we like about where we live, we do not think of its GDP per capita score, or its public expenditure ranking. We think of the multifarious things that make it satisfying, and few can yet be captured in the official statistics. Many efforts have been made to construct new measures of economic welfare which do justice to environmental and social dimensions of quality of life as well as to economic activity (Jackson 1998; Christie and Nash 1998; Jacobs, 1998).

It is a sign of the influence of such thinking, and also of environmentalist and feminist campaigns over recent decades, that the New Labour Government has made radical moves to supplement the mainstream economic indicators of policy making with much more varied and 'holistic' indicators of quality of life, at national, regional and local levels. Indicators of UK quality of life now include measures of the health of wild bird populations as well as of GDP growth and income. This move was accompanied by a striking acknowledgement by Tony Blair in his foreword to the Government's Sustainable Development Strategy:

> The last hundred years have seen a massive increase in the wealth of this country and the well being of its people. But focusing solely on economic growth risks ignoring the impact – both good and bad – on people and on the environment...Now...there is a growing realisation that real progress cannot be measured by money alone...But in the past, governments have seemed to

forget this. Success has been measured by economic growth – GDP – alone. We have failed to see how our economy, our environment and our society are all one. And that delivering the best possible quality of life for us all means more than concentrating solely on economic growth (DETR, 1999).

By the standards of most postwar governments in the West, this is a welcome and radical advance in thinking. But it has yet to be translated on a broad front into practical and effective policies. The greater the gap between the sentiments expressed in this vision of a new perspective for politics, and the realities of policy making and service design, the more an oppositional politics of quality of life can flourish.

The gap that exists between the policies of even a largely progressive government such as New Labour, and the concerns which fuel so many citizens' retreat from conventional politics and embrace of new campaigns and networks, is large. The Government has yet to acknowledge in full the implications of Tony Blair's frank statement that money, growth and economics are not enough. For the implications are radical: they point to profound challenges to prevailing priorities in consumption, work, production and decision making systems.

Quality of life as an idea relates to the sources of the 'satisfiers' in life – the factors which allow us to meet our needs and wants (Jackson and Marks 1998). Most obviously, there are material satisfiers – food, drink, clothing, shelter, and the whole cornucopia of consumer products and services which meet material needs and generate new types of desire. The satisfaction of private wants through personal consumption, made possible on an unprecedented scale by postwar capitalism, has been the dominant theme in policy makers' thinking about progress and living standards. But the focus of attention in quality of life debates in recent years has been on the sources of well-being which are rooted in the *public* realm.

A major element in the critique of prevailing priorities in consumption has been the argument that much of our quality of life depends not on the maximisation of private choices but on the collective goods supplied by society as a whole and by the environment. My private consumption depends on social goods – the public services that underpin everyday life – and on environmental ones – the water, air and soils that make up our 'life support systems'. It is precisely these that have been neglected in economic measurement, and – even more crucially – in the policy making climate of the last two decades, dominated as they have been by neo-liberal views of market forces and individualist models of choice and progress. The effect of the long development of consumer capitalism, individualism and the downgrading of the public sector by 'Thatcherism' has been to discount the contribution of the social and environmental *commons* to quality of life.

Quality of life depends not only on my private choices but also on the collective goods I need. I can privatise some of these to some extent – buying personal security, for example, by living in a 'gated community', or avoiding dependence on the public transport system by using my car at all times. But there are limits to private escape from dependence on what community and environment supply. I cannot avoid using the road network if I insist on using my car; and outside my gated community I cannot avoid some dependence on the social capital – the relations of trust, observation of the law and reciprocity – which underpins community life. If these collective goods decline in quality, then we all lose in quality of life, even if the rich can buy some space and time to insulate themselves from many of the effects. Sooner or later, the space of 'I' has to shade into that of 'we'.

Moreover, the potential that 'I' have for thriving depends on the quality of the realm which only 'We' can make collectively. Yet this is not to argue that all improvements to public goods always make everyone better off: they do not. Paying for them requires taxation which represents an opportunity cost to those who contribute money but do not make much or any use of particular public services. 'Quality of life' arguments for more investment in environmental protection and social goods cannot simply appeal to the idea that these things all benefit individuals and that reduced private consumption in favour of greater collective investment will inevitably be experienced as a gain in personal well-being. We have to want collective goods because they make for a better society, regardless of the direct impact on our personal quality of life (Jacobs 1997). The politics of quality of life stands on the principle that society exists and matters, over and above the well-being of individuals and families. To the extent that it is emerging as a key strand in millennial politics, it represents a rejection of the hard-core individualist idea at the heart of neo-liberalism.

Limits to 'choice': the core issues

There are other dimensions to the issue of quality of life that have increased its salience in today's politics.

Consumer control: the imbalance in individuals' lives

Much market research stresses the gains in 'consumer power' over the last two decades, as companies have increasingly sought to tailor their offers to affluent households and individuals and as consumer choices have proliferated for those who can afford them. Governments have encouraged the notion that 'the consumer is king', and there is a well-documented increase in propensity among consumers to complain, assert their rights, gain confidence in dealing with retailers, and experiment with different offers. But this all comes with two important price tags. First, the proliferation of choice does not always bring a sense of control: many consumers now experience 'choice' in shops as a source of frustration, unease and confusion

(Henley Centre, 2000). Second, and more important, what sense of control we have as *consumers* is in many cases wholly out of kilter with what we experience as *citizens, workers, parents, friends and spouses*. In all of these areas, our choices and sense of control may be extremely limited. As citizens, we have infrequent and often unsatisfying opportunities to influence governance through voting and giving voice to arguments. As workers, we may well experience constraint, lack of opportunity or oppressive demands that squeeze the time we can make available to our families and friends. As parents, we find that the pressures of work – or of lack of work and money – erode the quality and quantity of time and energy we bring to family life. The syndrome is one of being in control as a consumer and out of control in the other realms of life (Henley Centre 1997).

The workplace and the home

This is related to the emerging debate on the 'work/life balance' – the complex cluster of emotions and attachments to work on the one hand and family and friends on the other (Wilkinson, 2000). This debate has been fostered by researchers, campaign groups, feminists and the media, and arouses extreme unease among policy makers, business and politicians. The attachment to work at the expense of the rest of life is evident in the political world and the failure of New Labour to do much to follow through with its pledges to reform the anti-social working patterns of the House of Commons, and in the ill-at-ease response of the Prime Minister to pressure to take paternity leave on the birth of his son in 2000.

Time is, as mentioned earlier, a core 'private good': it is eroded by public demands, above all from the world of work, which is also embraced as a source of private satisfactions in terms of careers, status, personal development, income and so on. The complex and rich debate within and beyond feminism on the limits to 'having it all' and the scope for work to provide women or men with satisfactions that can either be reconciled with, or compensate for the lack of, home life, has still to make a breakthrough in mainstream politics. So far the debate has been propelled by women, and many men have remained outside it, reluctant to acknowledge limits to their own experience of work as a private good, or to admit that they actually prefer the workplace to the home. But as workplace demands become more intense in many areas (Burchell 1999), and the pressure on men – and from men – to make a full contribution to family-raising grows, so the divergence of interests between men and women in this dimension of quality of life politics could narrow. We could see more pressure coming from men for resistance to work intensification practices in organisations, and more desire among businesses and public bodies to collaborate with workers and childcare organisations to devise family-friendly innovations in work practice, as they seek to retain key staff at all levels of skill.

But this set of issues extends beyond the obvious clashes between home life and workplace priorities. It reminds us of the argument, presented by Daniel Bell in the 1970s, that capitalism generates its own 'cultural contradictions' (Bell 1978). Companies need workers who will follow the disciplines of the business and commit themselves to its needs. But they also need balanced, healthy, 'emotionally literate' and reasonably contented people. What if the individualist consumerism on which businesses depend produces people unable to operate in teams, or to discipline themselves, or to think properly of others' needs? What if the routines and disruptions of the workplace demand that our workers are different people in the business world from the kind of people we need them to be in the home? Richard Sennett has recently renewed this argument, making the case that the demands of the 'flexible' workplace in the 1980s and 1990s have eroded the social capital of work and corroded the 'character-building' role of stable workplaces. This is detrimental to the workplace as a 'commons' and to social relations generally (Sennett, 1998). The world of work as presently organised can undermine individual and collective quality of life.

This perspective connects the idea of 'having it all' to the public realm of work. So far, the debate on the benefits and downsides of work as opposed to family life has focused on the discovery by many women that careers do not offer as many satisfactions as expected, and are hard to combine with having children and raising them well. But this skews the debate and places most of the burden of trade-offs and dilemmas as to priorities on women. We still need a richer debate that draws in men and focuses on the limits to their aspirations to 'have it all' in the world of work and home life.

And beyond that, the debate needs to embrace more organisations, including government bodies, going further in challenging the work practices and management ethos that have sought to colonise ever more time among their employees – a corporate version of 'having it all' which has consequences not only for the private quality of life of workers but also for society in so far as it damages family life and trust between workers and employers. The Government's failure to reform the absurd working practices and hours of the House of Commons is symptomatic of a wider reluctance to face up to the contradictions and tensions in its desire to see both a more productive and flexible, meritocratic and hard-working labour force and also to foster stable and healthy families. Part of the answer – as with the efforts now underway to find techniques to value the services provided by the natural environment – must be to look for better ways of valuing the services provided by parents and households, and the work of raising families. At present, the work-life debate is marked by the imbalance between our multiple forms of valuing work and our reluctance to recognise the labour of family life as a contribution to society which needs to be awarded greater recognition and social and economic value (Wilkinson 2000). (This in turn is part of a much wider argument of relevance to the politics of quality of life: why do we see progress from 'welfare to work' as being exclusively a movement into conventional paid work, and why can we not also recognise better forms of social contribution such as caring and volunteering?)

The influential US 'ideas entrepreneur' Jeff Gates offers a resonant twist on this argument. He asks: Do we have a capitalism that acts 'as if children mattered'? (Gates, 1998) If company cultures undermine family life, and if they undermine the environment, then they are eroding capitalism's own capacity to sustain itself and deliver the goods we want from it. The system has enormous reserves of energy and innovative capacity, but it runs ahead of people's ability to adapt except at the expense of wider social relations. It thus contributes to what Fukuyama calls the 'miniaturisation of community' – the specialisation and attenuation of individuals' social networks under pressures of time, work and personal interest (Fukuyama 1999). Even more problematic for the long-run health of the system, its innovative power runs far ahead of our capacity to understand the impact of its resource use on the environment, and ahead of the environment's capacity to absorb wastes and adapt to changes wrought by human action. This perspective connects us to the next key issue in the politics of quality of life – the environmental and social limits to present forms of growth.

Environmental and social limits to choice

Two 'big ideas' from the 1970s return with a vengeance in the millennial politics of quality of life. First, the notion of the environmental limits to growth and consumer choice has become more relevant as our awareness of the degradation of local and global environments has grown. The 1970s analysis of 'limits to growth' was much too crude, focusing on the exhaustion of stocks of natural resources. But the new analysis, which focuses on the limits to natural systems' *tolerance* of growth in pollution, waste and consumption of key resources (such as fish stocks, fossil fuels), suggests an urgent need to curb our consumption in some respects and redirect it in more environmentally sustainable ways (UNEP, 1999). It is now evident, and reflected in ever more areas of policy making and business planning, that growth in fossil fuel-intensive production and consumption cannot continue, and that many forms of consumption impose unsustainable costs on the environment (demand for cheap, intensively produced food, for example). Again, we see here a mismatch between important forms of individual choice and the quality of the commons on which we depend.

Second, the idea of the social limits to growth has re-emerged. This was popularised by Fred Hirsch, who analysed the ways in which growth in demand for 'positional goods' could not be accommodated indefinitely (Hirsch, 1978). Positional goods, unlike mass market goods, decline in quality the more people try to gain access to them – homes with a lakeside view, holidays in 'unspoiled' places, the freedom of the road in your car. The rise of road rage is a sign that we are approaching the limits to growth in car use, and in the process damaging the collective commons – social and environmental – as well as our personal quality of life.

These factors redirect attention to the ways in which personal 'choice' in consumption can become destructive and indeed self-defeating. The UK debates on the location of new housing, and on the need to restrain car use, highlight the problems. People want the positional goods of rural homes and free use of the road, but not the consequences of other people's consumption of the same goods (Christie and Jarvis, 1999). And politicians, fearful of consumers' reaction to constraints on cherished forms of consumption, shy away from honest debate about the limits to present consumption and the need for new collective solutions.

Moreover, multiple perverse consequences can arise. The phenomenon of the 'school run' provides a good illustration. The more we use our cars, the more parents fear the risks to their children in walking or cycling to school. So they drive children to school, thus increasing the perceived risk of walking and boosting pressure on other parents to escort their children by car. The growth in traffic increases the risk of accidents, adds to pollution (including risk of asthma afflicting children), restricts children's exercise and adds to risks of ill-health as a result, adds to the congestion on the roads from commuter traffic, restricts further the effectiveness of bus transport, and imposes considerable time costs on adults. Indeed, the school run is a feminist issue. Jonathan Gershuny has shown that escorting children is a significant factor in restricting women to part-time work (Gershuny, 1993). The school run illustrates the self-defeating nature of some key forms of personal choice, and the ways in which these generate problems which can only be resolved through new forms of *collective* decision making, choice and consumption. As Ken Worpole notes:

> Thus the means compromise the ends. The result is that 'safe routes to school' programmes encouraging children to walk to school are now being set up round the country, and so walking becomes a radical – even innovative! – solution to a complex problem...We are surrounded by the problems caused by the wealth of choices available to us in a consumer economy, ranging from how we reconcile the desire to live in a semi-rural setting, with good schools and pleasant neighbours in close proximity, with the wishes of millions of others to do exactly the same; or the belief that we can somehow have a plentiful supply of cheap food and fashionable clothing while closing our eyes to the conditions of the animals bred in battery farms, or the wages and conditions of young children who work in sportswear factories in the developing world. (Worpole, 1999)

Distributional issues make a return to politics in this perspective on quality of life. The moment we envisage limits to key forms of consumption – such as private car use – we need to pay renewed and careful attention to the issues of equity which arise. How do we devise forms of 'rationing' of use of the commons (such as the roads) which do not penalise the poor, or those dependent on car use in rural areas? These factors point us towards a large-scale reinvestment in public goods – such as the public transport infrastructure – as a precondition for placing limits on consumption of resources when access to them is unevenly distributed.

Conscience, connectedness and the quality of life

The complexity of the connections noted by Ken Worpole underlines a major new feature of quality of life politics. The latest phase of globalisation has hugely expanded the connections between the rich and poor worlds, and also the range of consumer choices available to affluent households in the West. We have consumed largely in ignorance of the environmental and social costs attached to the production of the goods and services we desire. But the rise of global media and NGOs have made the world of consumption an 'x-ray' environment in which these costs will invariably be uncovered and brought to our often unwilling attention (Elkington 1997). Global connectedness means a new network of moral linkages as well as new supply chains, markets and choices. This is not simply a matter of business practices, of the regulation of multinational firms and their policies in the poor world. It relates directly to the expansion of consumer choices. These can be used to exert leverage for good, as in the growth of the Fair Trade movement and in pressure on firms such as Nike to reform their labour practices in South East Asia. But they can also lock whole communities in the developing world into forms of bondage – as with the drug economies that supply Western demand, based on ruthless exploitation of peasant labour and diversion of energies from food and other crop production. Individual choices can connect us to global chains of supply and demand, exploitation and inequality, which pose complex problems of collective response: as consumers, we can exert control over choices. But if we find that these choices trouble us, we have limited control in our role as individual economic agents. We can only make ethically and environmentally better choices through *collective* action.

A case in point is the 'globalisation of care', analysed in a powerful essay by Arlie Russel Hochschild, who brilliantly draws attention to the web of connections linking individuals – usually women – in 'global care chains' (Hochschild, 2000). The decision by an affluent woman in the US to hire a Filipino nanny and housekeeper is not a discrete consumer choice sealed off from wider connections. Who cares for the nanny's children back home? It may be a mother, who in turn must leave care of her children to an older daughter. Should the mother in the US care about the welfare of the children at the end of the chain, and other mothers' access to care? If not, why not? Hochschild highlights the degree to which these connections are obscured in political debate and discussion of the work-life balance and economics of child care: as she notes, 'We live global but feel local'. Can we make these global care chains benign, a force for progress in Asia at the end of the network of links as well as a convenient solution to a problem in the rich world? Her analysis concludes that 'the personal is global' – an echo of the old feminist line that the 'personal is political'.

Again, we see here how the politics of quality of life brings questions of justice and distribution, suppressed by the consensus politics of economic growth, back into the heart of debate. In the absence of a collective response to the tension between private wants and public goods, as in the case of the work-life imbalance, it is the affluent who are best positioned to make private provision which can restore to them some control over time and work. But this is often bought through low-paid childcare and imposition of a 'flexible' working framework on poor women, who in turn may be subjected to the pressures of time squeeze on their own lives as family carers as well as on their income and control of their working arrangements. Only through a more collective response – as envisaged in the Government's long term vision of affordable and accessible childcare – can a fair resolution or management of the tensions be achieved.

Asking about purpose: quality of life and decision making

The politics of growth and economic management is a politics of process. Governments have had all kinds of outcomes in mind for particular policies, of course, but have over recent decades and especially since the end of the Cold War retreated from the idea that societies should have a vision of their purposes, a grand plan. This has a healthy basis: the 20th century's key examples of societies with a vision of their destiny at the heart of their politics have been repulsive and bloodstained. But the West has arguably gone too far down the road of 'non-judgemental' liberalism. Democracies have focused their energies on honing the process of economic growth: their goals are to keep the show on the road and perpetuate growth and choice for consumers. Political purposes are to do largely with finding more effective ways to deliver growth and spread its benefits: it is up to individuals to have visions and search for meaning in life. But this approach is reaching its limits. If the above analysis is right, then these goals will need to be adjusted in radical ways, changing the patterns of production and consumption to reverse environmentally and socially unsustainable trends. We cannot duck the question of what purposes growth and the economy serve. They are, after all, means and not ends – something obscured in much political debate which focuses on growth and choice as ends in themselves.

Politicians who persist in seeing growth uncritically as an end, rather than as a means, risk losing contact with the public as more citizens shift their concerns to the terrain of the politics of quality of life. The crisis over GM foods is a sharp illustration of this risk. In the US and UK, decision makers in business and government identified GM technology as a valuable innovation – it would make money, increase efficiency in food production, boost biotechnology enterprise, and potentially help solve serious environmental and social problems. But their approach ignored the moral dimension of the choice to deploy GM technologies, and public concerns over the motivation behind it and the implications of experiments going wrong. GM foods, far from being another innovation serving growth, to be welcomed with few reservations, became a symbol of *hubris* in politics and business, a sign that growth was being served regardless of wider considerations of moral purpose and environmental impact. Moreover, here was an illustration of the personal – choices over food – becoming political, and of politics ignoring personal choice. Worse, once again, we saw an issue where individual choice could not establish control for the consumer: for GM foods can contaminate the food chain and make a mockery of labelling schemes. Only *collective* processes could produce a good result for the consumer. The personal is political, but the solutions to the problems at the heart of this connection are *social* not individual.

Mechanisms have now been established to improve expert scrutiny of GM innovations and other biotechnology developments, as a result of the furore unleashed by NGOs, the media and concerned consumers in the UK and beyond. But will expert scrutiny be enough? One feature of the uproar over GM foods is the growing demand for new processes that will connect people better to decision making and increase the accountability of experts. Quality of life politics is about an expansion of control in our roles as citizens, workers, parents and friends. We need to reconnect these realms to that of the consumer. It is hard to see how this can be done through the prevailing mechanisms of representative democracy alone. The opportunities for feedback and decision making by individuals are too infrequent, and the loss of trust in established systems too great. Moreover, elected representatives are wary of the politics of quality of life: there are too many risks of offending key constituencies, of seeming to moralise about choices, or of entering a terrain which fits ill with normal political and departmental boundaries.

The politics of quality of life thus points to the need for new deliberative mechanisms, for example in the planning system at neighbourhood level, in which individuals can confront the wider consequences of their own choices and seek to resolve conflicts and generate consensus (Warburton, 1998; Healy, 1997; Worpole, 1999). Experimentation in participatory democracy is going on in many places, a key indicator of the shift in political culture at the grassroots.

They are a way of opening up debate on *long term issues of demand management and limits to consumption as usual* which our 'short-termist' democratic systems fight shy of tackling for fear of losing key support from electors – such as managing demand for health care, or curbing demand for car use in congested cities. New forms of 'deliberative democracy' are emerging: citizens' juries, offering deliberation by lay citizens on tough issues which policy makers and politicians are wary of; deliberative polling exercises to develop public awareness of issues and assess how opinion changes as more information and ideas are absorbed; 'visioning' conferences, focusing citizens' attention on the future quality of life they would wish to see in the long term for their communities; 'roundtable' forums bringing interests together on common problems where collective solutions have been elusive; and the ambitious community mediation processes pioneered by NGOs such as Mediation UK and the Environment Council.

There has been great interest in citizens' juries and consensus conferences, in which a jury of citizens learns about a complex issue over a number of days, is able to examine expert witnesses, and (it is hoped) reaches a consensus on policy options. The low levels of public turnout for local elections have spurred efforts to devise innovations in the decision making process in areas such as local land use planning, to give citizens more sense of 'ownership' and 'empowerment' in local democracy. There has also been a widespread use of community 'visioning' events, often as part of Local Agenda 21 initiatives at the district level of government, to identify citizens' long-term concerns and priorities for their neighbourhoods. Citizens' juries and consensus conferences have been used to develop ideas about such complex issues as rationing of public health care services, disposal options for nuclear waste, and the development of genetically modified foods (Coote and Lenaghan, 1996).

As the planner Patsy Healey has argued, focusing on *local* quality of life and environmental issues can be the key to revitalising trust and engagement with the democratic process, and to reconnecting excluded groups and communities to governance and hope of shaping a better life:

> movement in the direction of inclusionary, collaborative planning should help to improve the quality of life for the many cultural communities in a place; to add material value not just to the companies in a place, but to those who share the experience of living there, and to work out how to act to sustain the critical biospheric capacities of a place. These benefits arise through the deliberative work of collaborative capacity-building, not through encouraging individualistic competitive behaviour (Healey 1997).

An opening for environmentalism and feminism?

The politics of quality of life rests on a new salience of connections between the personal and political, consumption and citizenship, work and family. It opens up significant opportunities for the two major social movements of the postwar period, environmentalism and feminism. Both have achieved important changes in the law and in the wider system of policy making in government and business. But both have struggled to connect with the mass of citizens. Environmentalists remain perceived by politicians and large sections of the public as 'anti-progress', and the complexity of many environmental messages is easily lost in the cut and thrust of normal political debate and media packaging of arguments. Feminism too, despite having entered the political atmosphere and shaped a whole climate of feeling, lacks the vocabulary and vision to inspire new generations of supporters. And both movements, extremely diverse by now, lack political voice outside the NGOs and grassroots campaigns which have achieved so much.

Quality of life politics opens up opportunities to create coalitions of support for both, and to connect both movements. For environmentalists, the language of quality of life is a way to emphasise that environmental reform of production and consumption can make us better off in many ways, material and non-material. While some 'sacrifices' are needed – such as less car use – the gains in quality of life will outweigh them. The argument also connects Green perspectives to social campaigners: reforms will improve the social conditions of the poorest people, who are most exposed to pollution, bleak environments and health risks. It emphasises that as individual consumers we have an interest in social goods that benefit 'us', even if they do not directly benefit 'me' (Jacobs, 1997). There is such a thing as society, and individuals need it. Increasingly, damage to the social and environmental commons can be shown to damage our personal lives and choices. Similar arguments animate the emerging debates on the work-life relationship and the direct and indirect gains to companies from a healthy and well-balanced ecology of family life and social relationships (Wilkinson, 2000).

Finally, in the developing politics of local quality of life, regeneration and 'sustainable communities' there is a need for far more attention to the gender dimension of care for the social and environmental commons, and this opens up ground on which environmentalists and feminists can meet each other and create new networks with citizens and community groups. Much of the work of repair and maintenance and use of the local commons is 'women's work', done by mothers above all; it is women who are most able to make the connections between personal 'choice' and local damage to quality of life, between the school run and the lack of public transport and safe streets, between the rundown parks and the growth of vandalism and fear of crime (Worpole, 1998). At the last election, a woman wrote to the *Guardian* to lament her lack of real choice as a citizen in the midst of ever-growing consumer choice: she wanted to be able to 'choose' good public transport, decent child care facilities, cleaner streets and safer public spaces. But these 'choices' can only be made by citizens via politics, not by consumers; and if politics-as-usual cannot help deliver them, then it will be rejected and reinvented. On such a slow and tortuous process we now seem to be embarked.

The potential of 'quality of life' to become the terrain on which a new politics of the environment, workplace and social life can be developed is enormous. It will not happen easily, for the issues are complex and hard to articulate within the frameworks of 'normal' politics and the priorities of those who dominate it – still largely men. Nor will the emergence of more political debates geared to the key quality of life issues guarantee that the 'right' answers will be found. We may discover that more open argument and mainstream debate on sustainable consumption leaves most citizens unmoved, and that the hunger for a better work-life balance is not as deep as we think it is. We might find that people prefer to avoid facing up to the trade-offs between private consumption and the quality of public goods as long as they can, until, for example, an overwhelmingly urgent crisis afflicts the environmental commons. But we might find that a politics which faces up to the issues of quality of life honestly and which finds new language and processes through which to do so, has the capacity to renew the link between citizens and governance, and between private consumption and the public good.

However, a major barrier to further progress in opening up the debates in the mainstream of politics is evident. While environmentalism and feminism have been successful in changing legislation and some attitudes at the top of business and politics, and in mobilising grassroots campaigns, they have been poor at *institution-building*. This has two aspects. First, there is a need to establish a strong political voice at the heart of mainstream politics, whether in the shape of political parties or powerful policy commitment in the existing parties. Second, there is a need to create or reform decision making processes that encourage the development of quality of life politics, and to generate systematic debates and forms of civic education and public engagement that begin to place the emerging tensions and prospective solutions at the heart of political argument. The politics of quality of life points to a need for environmentalists and feminists to work together, and with local communities, businesses and politicians in the design of participatory mechanisms that can become routine features of the landscape, rather than marginal and optional ones. These could include citizens' juries and consensus-building forums, reformed mechanisms for public engagement in land use planning, and better systems for securing community participation in the design and management of regeneration programmes at neighbourhood level. In addition, new forms of corporate reporting and public dialogue could be introduced in the business sector – engaging workers, families and local 'stakeholder' communities – on the social and environmental impacts of a company's operations. And new collective solutions could be developed to quality of life problems, such as safe-routes-to-school projects, workplace car-pooling schemes, workplace nurseries and creches, job-sharing schemes, and Fair Trade initiatives linking rich and poor countries.

Such initiatives, though local and unglamorous, would signal that the politics of quality of life is moving from the margins towards the centre of 21st century decision making. They offer a new vocabulary and toolkit to environmentalists and feminists among others. More important, they point to a more connected and richer life for all of us, not just as consumers, but as citizens, workers and family members. The rediscovery of the social and environmental commons and their connection to our individual choices is the quiet revolution of our time.

References:

Bell D (1979) *The Cultural Contradictions of Capitalism* New York: Basic Books.

Burchell B *et al* (1999) *Job Insecurity and Work Intensification* York: Joseph Rowntree Foundation

Christie I and Nash L (eds) (1998) *The Good Life* London: Demos.

Christic I and Jarvis L (1999) 'Rural spaces, urban jams' in Jowell R *et al* (eds) *British Social Attitudes* Aldershot: NCSR/Ashgate.

Coote A and Lenaghan J (1997) *Citizens' Juries: Theory into Practice* London: IPPR.

DETR [Department for Environment, Transport & Regions] (1999) *A Better Quality of Life* London: Stationery Office

Elkington J (1997) *Cannibals with Forks* London: Capstone

Frank R and Cook P (1995) *The Winner Take All Society* New York: Free Press.

Fukuyama F (1992) *The End of the History and the Last Man* London: Hamish Hamilton, London.

Fukuyama F (1999) *The Great Disruption* London: Profile.

Galbraith J K (1992) *The Culture of Contentment* London: Penguin.

Gates J (1998) *The Ownership Solution* London: Allen Lane.

Gershuny J (1993) 'Escorting children: impact on parental lifestyle' in Hillman M (ed) *Children, Transport and the Quality of Life* London: Policy Studies Institute.

Giddens A (1991) *Modernity and Self-Indentity* Cambridge: Polity Press.

Healey P (1997) *Collaborative Planning* London: Macmillan

Henley Centre (1997) *Planning for Social Change 98* London: Henley Centre.

Henley Centre (2000) www.henleycentre.com

Hirsch F (1978) *Social Limits to Growth* London: Routledge

Hochschild A R (2000) 'Global Care Chains and Emotional Surplus Value' in Hutton W and Giddens A (eds) *On the Edge: living with global capitalism* London: Cape.

Jackson T *et al* (1998) *An Index of Sustainable Economic Welfare for the UK 1950-96* Guildford: Centre for Environmental Strategy, University of Surrey.

Jackson T and Marks N 'Found Wanting?' (1998), in Christie I and Nash L (ed) *op cit.*

Jacobs M (1997) 'The quality of life' in Jacobs M (ed) *Greening the Millennium?* Oxford: Blackwell

Mulgan G and Wilkinson H (1995) *The Time Squeeze* London: Demos

Sennett R (1998) *The Corrosion of Character* New York: Norton.

Warburton D (ed) (1998) *Community and Sustainable Development* London: Earthscan

Warburton D (1999) *Your Place and Mine: reinventing planning* London: TCPA

Wilkinson H (ed) (2000) *Family Business* London: Demos.

Worpole K (1998) 'Bottle banks in Arcadia' in Warburton D (ed) (1998) *op cit.*

Worpole K (1999) 'Path not (yet) taken: the politics of sustainability' in Worpole K (ed) *Richer Futures* London: Earthscan.

UNEP (1999) *Global Environment Outlook 2000* London: Earthscan.